# chili
# from the
# southwest

# chili from the southwest

## fixin's, flavors, and folklore

### W. C. JAMESON

taylor trade publishing

Lanham • New York • Dallas • Boulder • Toronto • Oxford

Published by Taylor Trade Publishing
An imprint of The Rowman & Littlefield Publishing Group, Inc.
4501 Forbes Boulevard, Suite 200
Lanham, Maryland 20706

Distributed by National Book Network

Library of Congress Cataloging-in-Publication Data

Jameson, W. C., 1942–
  Chili from the Southwest : fixins, flavors, and folklore / W. C. Jameson.—1st Taylor Trade
Pub. ed.
      p. cm.
  ISBN 1-58979-244-0 (pbk. : alk. paper)
  1. Chili con carne. 2. Cookery, American—Southwestern style.  I. Title.
  TX749.J34 2005
  641.8'236—dc22                                                    2005011617

# contents

# foreword

Chili is Texas food with a Spanish accent.

Like many things considered Texan (much of cowboy lingo, for instance), chili has its origins in the Hispanic community, and usage gradually evolved into something different and new. It continues to evolve, expanding both its base and its variety.

Chili came into its own during the early part of the twentieth century. It and hamburgers helped many a poor man survive the long years of the Great Depression. Both were relatively cheap and could sustain life if need be. Chili certainly had more body to it than soup, especially when thickened with enough crumbled-up saltine crackers. Its simplicity made it a favorite of bachelors surviving on their own cooking. Many an old chuckwagon cook, too stove up to stay out on the range any longer, set up shop in town as proprietor of a chili joint.

Chili is highly flexible. It can be made hot as a branding iron or mild as a spring morning, depending on the cook's personal preference and the demands of his or her clientele. Its primary ingredient is meat. It can be made out of anything that eats grass or lays eggs. Though beef is usually the first choice, goat is a common ingredient in South Texas. Mutton is permissible in sheep country. Wild game is always good and allows the cook to brag about his marksmanship. Chicken is a little over the edge, but there's no law against it. Fish probably carries a penitentiary sentence.

Chili would be just beef stew if it were not for peppers to add that special tang, plus garlic, onions, cumin, and oregano to arrive at its distinctive flavor. Peppers come in countless varieties and all levels of self-contained heat to test the consumer's fire resistance.

As W. C. Jameson says in this book, chili has become a Texas icon. More than that, it has become almost a religion with enthusiasts who flock to competitive cook-offs from the Midwest to California. Secret recipes are as jealously guarded as plans for the atomic bomb. Fistfights have been known to erupt between those who advocate adding beans to their chili and purists who insist that it is blasphemy akin to spitting on the churchhouse floor. Red beans add body and go a long way toward satisfying hunger, but lots of chiliheads maintain that this is like compromising the purity of a good woman. If beans must be served, they say, put them in their own bowl.

The ultimate Texas chili celebration is the annual blowout at the old ghost town of Terlingua near the Big Bend National Park. There, all manner of extroverts and wanna-be comedians stage an exuberant exhibition and, incidentally, cook up enough chili to put the Rio Grande on a two-foot rise. It is safe to say that brewery stock advances several points during the blowout. A little beer even makes its way into the chili.

I must admit that as a boy growing up on a ranch near Crane, Texas, I heard about chili a lot more often than I got a chance to taste it. Despite its reputation as a staple of ranch fare, it only occasionally surfaced at the McElroy Ranch. On those occasions when Mother served it, she usually got it from a can of Wolf Brand. That is no disparagement of Wolf Brand, whose motto used to be "How long has it been since you had a hot, steaming bowl of Wolf Brand chili? Well, that's too long."

I thought it tasted pretty dern good. Still do.

I often heard that chili was a staple of chuckwagon menus, but I don't remember the McElroy cooks fixing it much. They leaned more toward what was euphemistically termed "son of a gun" stew. Around the wagon it was more often "son of a bitch," and sometimes "gentleman from Odessa." Teacher and folklorist Paul Patterson said he used to wonder why it was called that until he *met* a gentleman from Odessa.

In recent years, chili has become a staple in the Kelton home during winter months. In a house where the central heating system leaves much to be desired, chili heats from the inside, satisfying the taste buds and warding off the common cold.

In hindsight, it is almost unbelievable that fundamentalist churches in McKinney, Texas, once campaigned to have chili outlawed on grounds that it was a sinful indulgence, the soup of the devil. Good chili has been described as a preview of heaven. At its extreme, it can provide a foretaste of the alternative.

In that light, it is akin to a sermon.

Elmer Kelton

# a bowl o' red

Love is like a bowl of chili: The hotter the better.

—Anonymous

Chili con carne can be, and often is, different things to different people, even different cultures. To some, chili is just a dish, a meal, nothing more than a bowl of spicy food. To others, it is primarily a topping for hot dogs. But to those who hold this special food in high regard, chili con carne represents an experience that can blend elements of history, geography, the culinary arts, and recreation.

Among purists, the preparation and consumption of chili have been elevated to an art form. Many consider cooking and eating chili a form of recreation; some regard it as a type of therapy. Chili cook-offs and parties are now a common and widespread form of entertainment that includes costumes and music. To a rapidly growing number of chilimeisters, cook-offs represent an opportunity for competition and provide a level of culinary excitement not encountered with most foods. There are even some who regard chili as an aphrodisiac, and a few have claimed eating a good bowl of red is akin to a spiritual experience.

Margaret Cousins, the venerable editor at Doubleday books years ago, once stated that "chili is not so much a food as a state of mind." Harry James, the famous bandleader and trumpet player, and a man who knew his chili, said, "Next to jazz music, nothing lifts the spirit and strengthens the soul more than a good bowl of chili." Francis X. Tolbert, a Texan long associated with chili, wrote, "A bowl of chili is a haunting, mystical thing."

Chili con carne has diffused from its original points of origin into a variety of different cultures, with its form and content modified along the way. But chili, real chili as it is perceived by serious chili cooks, serious chili eaters, and even chili scholars, is so much more than mere food. This special dish, in its many forms and in so many different ways, has become part and parcel of the culture of North America as well as some other parts of the world.

The late, great humorist Will Rogers loved chili con carne and spoke of it often. Rogers rated the quality of life in towns around the United States on the basis of the chili found in each one. His simple survey was a forerunner of today's popular places-rated surveys. Rogers' only criterion for rating a place, however, was the chili. According to him, Coleman, Texas, was at the top of the list.

To the devoted, a good bowl of chili is all of these things and more. Well-prepared, authentic chili, according to the believers, transcends everything and truly becomes, as suggested by Cousins, a state of mind.

Food historians are in near-complete agreement that chili has its origins in Texas, though other locations also claim the honor. During its formative years and early evolution, chili was beef (chopped or cubed), peppers (anchos or pequins, pulped or crushed), garlic (minced or chopped), cumin, oregano, and salt. All was cooked together and allowed to simmer for at least a couple of hours. Chili purists today vary little, if at all, from this tried-and-true recipe.

The inevitable craving for chili eventually began spreading beyond its point of genesis during the late 1800s. Regional cultures sometimes modified the dish on the basis of available ingredients and taste preferences or just to experiment with the basic recipe. Over time, some found adding certain ingredients to their liking: onions, tomatoes, cayenne, thyme, beer, and broth. Still others have gone to what the traditionalists regard as unnecessary extremes by adding such nontraditional ingredients as celery, bell peppers, beans, tequila, whiskey, sugar, and even spaghetti! Those who like a thick chili often add flour, masa harina, cracker meal, and even oatmeal. Devotees of thinner chili add various kinds of liquid ranging from water to canned juices to almost any kind of hard liquor, including whiskey, bourbon, vodka, brandy, and schnapps.

Nutritionists are now giving chili a second look and finding some good things to say about it. As a food, chili, if prepared correctly, can be good for a person. Trimmed of fat and cooked in a high-quality olive oil, the meat provides necessary protein. The peppers traditionally used in chili are rich in vitamins A and C. According to folklore and contemporary practice, these peppers have been used to treat a number of conditions including toothaches, gout, colic, ague, seasickness, colds, sore throats, and dropsy. Chile peppers have been known to aid digestion and clarify the blood. According to physicians, a regular diet of chiles helps rid the body of fats, lowers cholesterol levels, and reduces the possibility of heart attack. Several studies have shown that regular consumers of chile peppers, such as Southwestern Indians and Mexicans, generally experience a lower incidence of heart disease than do most Americans.

Chili may also be the most misunderstood food in America, if not the entire world. Many believe chili is a Mexican food, a notion fostered by inaccurate references in cartoons and movies. Chili con carne, though made with some ingredients that come from Meso-America, is a uniquely American dish, and some would argue uniquely Texan.

Many are also convinced that chili must be fiery hot. It can be, and often is, but doesn't need to be, and more often isn't. The chili served in authentic chili parlors across Texas and the American Southwest is spicy but seldom hot, and garnishes such as chile peppers and onions are generally available at the table so that the diner may adjust the flavor as desired. Arguments have been waged and fistfights fought over whether or not beans should be included in chili con carne, a debate that wages to this day. There even remains some confusion over the appropriateness of adding tomato to chili.

Chili con carne was once banned by fundamentalist churches as being Satanic. During the 1890s, chili was a relatively new dish and generally unknown outside of Texas. During the latter part of that decade, Myers' Café opened in the small town of McKinney, located several miles north of Dallas. The new café featured chili con carne, a decision that caused immediate controversy.

Several McKinney residents were leery of this somewhat unknown food and claimed it could ruin a person's insides. Testimony to that effect was solicited from physicians, sometimes concocted, and passed around as fact. Parents were soon forbidding their children to eat chili, claiming it would stunt their growth, cause disfigurement, and render them idiots. Then, as now, all one had to do to encourage a youngster to try anything was to forbid him to do so. In no time at all, the youth of McKinney were spending their allowances on bowls of chili down at Myers' Café. At all hours of the day, according to newspaper reports of the time, the tiny eatery was filled with boys from twelve to sixteen years of age gobbling up chili at twelve cents a bowl.

This kind of disobedience could not go unpunished. Angry letters began appearing in the McKinney newspaper describing the loose morals of the town's youth. Food was for sustenance, claimed one of the letter writers, not for enjoyment, and for a child to take so much pleasure from a simple bowl of food was an evil thing that could only lead him down the road to greater sins.

Soon McKinney's fundamentalist churches got into the act. Ever on the lookout for something to ban, many of the town's preachers were condemning chili from the pulpit and preaching sermons about the "sinful indulgence in a food that was prepared by Satan himself." In fact, for a long time in McKinney, chili was referred to as the "soup of the Devil."

All of this anti-chili ranting did little more than generate a keener interest and curiosity among normal people about this new and forbidden dish. As a result, soon there was standing-room-only at Myers' Café from morning until night, seven days a week, as McKinney citizens lined up to sample this youth-corrupting food. Some also reported that one or two of the town's fundamentalist preachers were actually spotted slurping up some of Satan's soup. Eventually, common sense intruded, and "the great chili furor," as it was called by newspaper columnist Francis X. Tolbert, died down.

Chili con carne remains controversial and misunderstood today for other reasons. In fact, there exists throughout the country a great deal of confusion about how it is spelled. According to chili scholars, the origin of the word may come from the Aztec Indians who thrived in Mexico around the time Columbus was visiting some of the Caribbean Islands. Over time, the word *chili* has become the only acceptable term, socially and culinarily, for the concoction of meat, peppers, and seasoning fans know and love today, the traditional "bowl o' red." An examination of the existing literature, however, as well as dozens of restaurant and café menus across the country, reveals multiple variations on the spelling of the word *chili*.

Sometimes *chile* is encountered. Chile, with an "e" at the end instead of an "i," refers specifically to peppers of the capsaicin family. The word *chile* is synonymous with the term *chile pepper*, whether red or green. These peppers, of course, are an essential ingredient in the making of chili.

The American South seems to offer the greatest variations in the spelling of this notable dish. South of the Mason-Dixon Line, I have found *chilli*, *chille*, *chilie*, *chillie*, and even *chililie*. In the Midwest, I have seen *chilly* and *chilley*. Once, while stopping for dinner at a roadside café in Iowa, I saw a menu listing for something called *chilly con carny*. Chili purists recommend never eating at places where the dish is not spelled correctly.

*Chili from the Southwest: Fixins, Flavors, and Folklore* offers the siftings of nearly four decades of research on the history, geography, and lore of chili, as well as more than 135 tested recipes. While the subject of food, and in particular chili, easily lends itself to an academic treatment, it is far too much fun to be dragged through a jungle of tedious jargon and cumbersome footnotes. Chili is to be enjoyed, not endured.

The recipes included in this book are the results of decades of searching, sampling, and experimenting. Some of those offered here are quite traditional; some were provided by friends and fellow chilistos, all kindred spirits of chiliana. Many were collected on the road during travels from border to border, coast to coast. A few originally came from old, long out-of-print cookbooks as well as from extant literature. Most have been modified over the years as a result of experimentation, from adding something here and deleting something else there, and from a variety of innovations inflicted from time to time.

A number of the recipes encountered herein are of my own design. All have been tried, kitchen- and banquet-tested, and ultimately developed into what is presented in these pages. My hope is that you enjoy preparing and dining on these recipes as much as I have enjoyed creating and working with them over the years.

One of the glories associated with the cooking and eating of chili, in addition to those mentioned previously, is that they are never-ending processes. No matter how perfect a recipe, the experimentation and the quest for a greater bowl of chili continues. Such culinary exploration and discovery remain worthwhile—indeed, noble—goals that I shall pursue until the last pepper is sliced.

The recipes included in this book have been divided into traditional chili and its variations, wild game chili, and fitness chili. The section on traditional chili recipes includes a number from winners of important competitions as well as some from celebrities such as James Arness, Marty Robbins, and Francis X. Tolbert. Chili has become a popular way to prepare and serve wild game, and chili con carne is almost a required meal in many autumn deer camps across the country. In response to a growing awareness of the values of healthy dining, the section on fitness chili provides a number of alternatives for those monitoring fat and cholesterol.

Chili con carne is one of the original fun foods, and that notion has certainly influenced the approach incorporated in this book. Chili can be nutritious and tasty, to be sure, but most of all chili is fun—the preparation, the tasting, and the ultimate serving of this noble and delectable dish to friends and loved ones at birthday parties, tailgate parties, fiestas, cookouts, hunting camps, and any other kind of gathering.

# the story of chili

Wish I had time for one more bowl of chili.

—Alleged last words of Kit Carson

Researching the history of chili con carne can be a rewarding yet in many ways a troublesome and difficult undertaking. The researcher encounters a multitude of earlier efforts, most of which yield a number of contradictory claims. As with most histories, the difficulties arise in trying to separate fact from fiction and, in some cases, fact from legend. As a result, the serious chili researcher winds up being confronted with a multitude of theories relating to the origin of the precious brew. Strong claims for any one of the theories can result in disagreements ranging from relatively quiet intellectual discussions to loud brawls. Each combatant remains steadfastly loyal to a particular theory and cannot be swayed by the opinions of others. Nor do the debaters seem to be in the least bit influenced by historical facts.

Ultimately, regardless of the specific theory of origin, who prepared the very first pot of chili will likely never be discovered. Chili, as fans know it and love it today, evolved over time and involved the contribution of a number of different cultures and individuals.

During the early settlement of Texas and the Southwest, a number of literate and observant explorers, soldiers, and others passed through the region: the French explorer Pages in 1767; Zebulon Pike in 1807; German scientist Roemer in 1846; the intrepid Frederick Law Olmstead in 1854; and Benjamin Lundy in 1883. Although E. DeGolyer, the millionaire and scholarly chilisto, once wrote that this unique dish was likely started during the 1840s, not a single one of the observant and curious individuals who traveled through Texas and the Southwest and who wrote about the environment, geology, people, wildlife, plants, resources, and food ever mentioned chili in his journals and reports. If chili had existed in the region, it surely would have been noted by these chroniclers.

In 1862, Confederate soldiers assigned to San Antonio reportedly grew boisterous in the city's plaza and wrecked a number of food stands. Although several different kinds of foods were mentioned as having been ruined, such as tamales and stews, there was not a single mention of chili. Around this same time, a visitor to San Antonio named Sidney Lanier wrote in detail of the wonders and delights of the city, but there was no mention of chili in his pages.

In 1874, *Scribner's* magazine published an article about San Antonio by Edward King. He wrote about a number of things including the great variety of food he encountered there, but chili was not among them. Joe Cooper once wrote about a painting by Thomas Allen, an artist who spent some time in San Antonio in 1879. Cooper notes that in one of Allen's paintings of the plaza, something that looks suspiciously like a chili stand is represented. During a journey through Texas in the early 1880s, two authors named Knox and Sweet wrote rather critically about Mexican, Texan, and Southwestern food, yet there was no mention of chili.

In 1882, however, *Gould's Guide to San Antonio* mentions chili con carne and its availability at various locations around the plaza. This, as far as I can determine, is the first official mention of chili in print. Many years later, somebody named Frank H. Buschick wrote a book that included an entire chapter on San Antonio's chili queens, the cooks and purveyors of freshly made chili. According to Buschick, the chili queens were in full operation in 1895.

In 1896, William Gebhardt began mixing the spices used in the making of chili and selling packets of them in San Antonio and throughout the surrounding area. Demand soon grew for his now famous chili powder, and by 1899, a full-fledged manufacturing and sales operation in the Alamo City existed.

In 1897, chili was mentioned again in print, this time in a novel titled *Wolfville* and authored by a man named Alfred Henry Lewis. In 1899, according to Cooper, a Mexican food restaurant opened in San Antonio that served, among other items, chili. The principal clientele were Americans. According to San Antonio lore, this is supposed to be the first Mexican food restaurant in the United States, though other cities and towns have had similar claims made for them.

The chronology pins down the origins of chili, more or less, to sometime between 1879 and 1882. Prevailing theories relative to the origins of chili have their supporters and detractors.

# the new world theory

Peppers, such as those employed in the preparation of chili, are native to that geographic region called Meso-America, a vast region consisting of Mexico, Central America, and most of northern South America. This area was home to Aztecs, Incas, Mayans, Quechuans, and other Indian tribes.

Archeological and anthropological records note that the natives of this region regularly dined on chile peppers mixed with meat and herbs, and they apparently did so for centuries prior to the arrival of the Spanish explorers. This dish, which clearly resembled chili as it is known today, was a staple food of the Meso-Americans, who, in turn, introduced it to the visiting Spaniards. The Spaniards, unfamiliar with the capsaiscin vegetables we call chiles today, confused them with the more familiar bell peppers. Mistakenly, they named the chiles "peppers," a name that has stuck over the ages.

Regardless of what the Europeans called the chiles, they certainly took a liking to this somewhat new and spicy food. As they continued their explorations and invasions throughout Meso-America and into what is now the United States, they carried along the ingredients and cooking techniques, probably adding a few of their own contributions to the pot now and again.

# the lady in blue theory

One claim for the early existence of what seems to be chili or something closely resembling it does, in fact, come from a provocative legend, which the Roman

Catholic church labels an old American Indian tale, that extends back to before the time of Spanish invasion and settlement in the western United States. A number of Southwestern Indian tribes told of being visited by a mysterious woman dressed entirely in blue. On these visits, according to the tale, she introduced the indigenes to the rudiments of Christianity and instructed them to prepare a glorious welcome for the eventual arrival of the Spanish missionaries. When the Spaniards finally came, they were mystified by all the stories about the lady in blue, whom they called *La Dama de Azul*. Missionary priest Alonso de Benarifes and the Spanish king Philip IV believed the lady in blue to be the spirit of Sister Mary of Agreda, who lived in a convent in Castile, Spain.

The story goes that Sister Mary entered the convent in 1618 when she was sixteen years of age. Not long afterward, she fell into a series of trances, some of which lasted for several days. When she finally recovered, she told of visiting a distant land where she walked among the natives and spoke to them about Christianity. With amazing accuracy, Sister Mary of Agreda described the landscape and inhabitants of the American Southwest and provided information about their language and foods. One particular dish she recorded consisted of venison, onions, tomatoes, and chile peppers, the earliest known recipe for what easily could be taken for, or mistaken for, chili.

# the Canary Islander theory

The Canary Islands are a Spanish possession located in the Atlantic Ocean a couple of hundred miles off the northwest coast of Africa. A popular theory holds that chili con carne was first concocted by immigrant Canary Islanders who arrived in San Antonio during the early 1700s. Canary Island cuisine was often characterized by the use of curry, but finding none of that seasoning in San Antonio, the newcomers substituted locally grown chile peppers as well as other herbs and seasonings, eventually creating a prototype of chili that no doubt resembled something they ate back home. The Canary Islander theory claims a high number of adherents and is one of the most often quoted in the available literature on the history of chili.

## the cultural mix theory

Another theory holds that chili may have been a dish that evolved simply as a result of the mixing of a variety of cultures that settled in San Antonio during the early to mid-1700s. Among these were the Canary Islanders, who were joined by Mexicans, a few French, and even some Italians and American Indians who resided there. As a result of the subsequent interaction, mixing, sharing, and borrowing, the dish called chili resulted, likely out of expediency.

## the missionary theory

Some believe chili con carne originated during the time of religious conversion of Indians in the American Southwest. According to writers Susan Hazen-Hammond and Eduardo Fuss, a Jesuit priest observed some natives preparing a stew consisting of chile peppers and meat all cooked together in lard. Hazen-Hammond and Fuss even included a recipe for this early "chili" in their book *Chile Pepper Fever: Mine's Hotter Than Yours*.

No one doubts the observations of the Jesuit priest, and likely the Indians had been preparing and eating this stew centuries before the missionaries ever showed up. Author and chilisto Joe Cooper offers a somewhat different point of view on the missionary theory. He suggests that the Jesuit priests themselves may have actually arrived at the recipe for chili as a means of stretching the meager food supplies, a situation that often existed at the early missions.

## the Texas army theory

Dogged researcher Joe Cooper also found a reference to a chili-like dish that had been assembled to feed the Texas army in 1835. According to Cooper, when military officials were mobilizing recruits in San Antonio, they needed to feed large numbers of people. Mexican cooks were hired to prepare whatever was available, which often turned out to be a hearty stew concocted from beef cooked with red chile peppers, a kind of prototypical chili.

## the Gold Rush theory

Some historians insist the origin of chili came much later than the Texas army, around the time of the California Gold Rush. Based on some rather scanty evidence provided by a man named E. DeGolyer, this theory suggests that during 1850, a party of Texans, while searching for an easy-to-prepare food they could quickly cook along the trail on their way to the California gold fields, came up with a mixture of beef, salt, black pepper, and chile peppers, all dried and carried in a tow sack. At dinner time, they simply broke off a piece of the mixture into a pot of boiling water and cooked it until it was ready to eat. If true, this could have been the first chili mix.

## the poor people theory

According to authors Maury Maverick Jr. and Charles Ramsdell, the poor people living in San Antonio invented chili sometime during the 1850s. Maverick stated that poor folks purchased inferior cuts of meat at low prices, cut them up into bite-sized pieces, cooked them in a pot until tender, and added chile peppers and onions for flavor.

## the Texas prison theory

This explanation for the genesis of chili also has its origins in Texas during the mid-1800s. In an effort to provide relatively nutritious meals at a low cost to criminals incarcerated in the state's prisons, somebody came up with a stew consisting of cuts of cheap and tough beef chopped into small cubes and mixed with chile peppers and a few spices. Though probably apocryphal, a story goes that this stew was reportedly so delicious that released and paroled prisoners, unable to obtain similar fare in the free world, committed crimes in order to be returned to prison and their jailhouse chili.

# the Texas cowboy theory

One of the most enduring theories, this explanation also seems to be one of the most quoted among a lot of chili historians, particularly those from Texas. Cowhands who were out rounding up cattle and driving them to the railheads in Kansas, Nebraska, and other points north during the 1860s and 1870s were in need of a filling, easy-to-prepare, stick-to-the-ribs type of fare to sustain them on their journey. Cooks often fixed stews on the trail simply because it was easy to do. The meals were prepared from cuts of beef accompanied by onions, herbs, and various seasonings. As one version of this story goes, a cook ran out of black pepper for the stew and allegedly added a handful of crushed red pepper from some chiles he found growing along the way.

# the San Antonio chili queen theory

Regardless of how chili originated and evolved, by the 1880s and 1890s, it was fairly well established throughout much of Texas and a few other parts of the American West and Southwest.

During the 1880s, a ubiquitous feature of many Texas cities, San Antonio in particular, was the presence of sidewalk chili vendors. The vendors, who were mostly women, spooned out bowls of hot, steaming chili to hungry customers on the plazas, squares, and streets. The chili queens, as they came to be called, went to great lengths to decorate their booths with elaborate designs and eye-catching colors to lure customers. Some even hired musicians to perform during business hours, a kind of precursor to the modern-day chili cook-offs.

For decades, the San Antonio chili queens served bowls o' red to thousands, if not millions, of people. Local merchants and laborers frequented the chili stands for lunch, and before long, these sidewalk chili vendors grew to become a cultural phenomenon and were often written about in travel magazines. Tourists to the Alamo City made visits to the booths a *de rigeur* stop. This extremely popular outdoor dining activity came to a screeching halt in

1943, however, when the city health officials shut down the chili queens, claiming unsanitary conditions.

However you interpret the history of chili, the clear consensus is that, while contributed to by other cultures, it is unquestionably American in origin. Even more specifically, chili in its traditional form was originally a Texas food. Arguments continue to rage, however, as to where in Texas this special cuisine had its beginnings. According to a vast number of passionate chili researchers, San Antonio has been generally recognized as the birthplace of the bowl o' red.

Another school of thought, one that claims equally passionate adherents, places the origins of chili con carne in the brush country of South-Central to Southwest Texas during the time of the vast cattle ranches and trail drives, where range cooks made do with what ingredients they had. The first chili, these fine folks claim, may very well have come from the back of a chuckwagon.

While demonstrably American and Texan in origin, chili would not be chili without some important ingredients borrowed from the Meso-Americans who provided chiles—anchos and others, fresh, crushed, and powdered—which had their origins in that region.

In spite of the overwhelming evidence that chili was birthed in the Lone Star State, many continue to believe it possesses a specific Mexican origin. A lot of people still labor under the misguided assumption that if a dish is spicy hot it must come from Mexico. This kind of false lore is perpetuated in film, cartoons, comics, and simple lack of culinary and dining experience. Many who pursue chili adventures around the hemisphere have traveled throughout much of Mexico and have encountered many varieties of delicious stews containing meat and chile peppers but have yet to find chili con carne as it exists today. Others who have traveled extensively throughout Mexico, Central America, and even South America claim they have never encountered a single bowl of chili at any of those locations.

Some who travel to Mexico and insist on dining at restaurants that cater exclusively to American tourists have reported finding chili con carne on the menus. There is a simple explanation: Mexican restaurant entrepreneurs are well aware that many Americans, as well as others who vacation south of the border, maintain certain expectations about food. Many, believing chili to be Mexican, expect to find it in their wanderings. As a result, Mexicans make chili and sell it, just as they do other kinds of Texas dishes such as fajitas and nachos.

Employing impeccable logic, Joe Cooper once wrote that if chili had come from Mexico it should still be found there. The truth is, chili con carne is rare in Mexico, seldom being found in cafés and restaurants and in the kitchens of the natives.

The role of the chili parlor has had an important influence on the evolution and dissemination of chili con carne. According to chili scholars, the chili parlor, an institution found today in numerous guises and incarnations around the country, also had its origins in Texas. During the 1920s and 1930s, many small-town Texas cafés, operating on a tiny budget, often offered chili and little else. These smallish cafés specializing in chili soon came to be known as chili parlors and evolved into important gathering places for local men and boys alike. Old men sat around eating chili, drinking coffee, discussing politics, and playing dominoes. Teenage boys talked about sports and about teenage girls. Business-men often found the chili parlors an ideal and inexpensive place to take a lunch break or feed a client.

Some early chili parlors sold a bowl o' red for around twenty-five cents, and it was generally accompanied by all the soda crackers a diner could eat. Chili parlors were responsible for introducing at least two generations of diners to this special dish.

As chili and chili parlors became important parts of the Texas culture, visi-tors and tourists discovered they liked this new and exciting dish called chili, even craved it and continued to yearn for it on returning to the North, Midwest, and East. As a result, the demand for chili began to grow in such far-flung loca-tions as Ohio, Illinois, and New York, and the geographic beginnings of an amazing cultural and culinary journey were underway.

TWO

# the geography
# of chili

In Texas, four things temporal are held inviolate—women, states'
rights, a cattle brand, and chili.

—Joe Cooper

Geography is a field of study that deals with a seemingly endless number of concepts including distance, direction, distribution, diffusion, cultures, acculturation, similarities, differences, and relationships. The study of foods clearly can be and often is geographical, and chili con carne in particular lends itself well to these kinds of investigations and interpretations. Through the science of geography, in fact, chili lovers can perhaps better understand the origins, evolution, diffusion, and modification of chili throughout a wide variety of cultures, many of which imposed their own regional tastes, needs, preferences, and tolerances onto this dish. Because of the ongoing and continuous changing and adjusting of the basic recipe for chili, this food varies markedly across the United States from culture to culture as much as or more than any other.

Chili possesses several geographic facets relative to its origins. Chile peppers are the result of the early plant domestication and agricultural pursuits of Mexican and Central American Indians. Generations of domestication and experimentation undertaken by Mayans, Incas, Aztecs, Quechuans, and other tribes yielded a variety of chiles that were often traded to tribes north of the Rio Grande in Texas and the American Southwest, where they quickly became established as a food item and an agricultural crop. The peppers also found their way into the Caribbean Islands.

When Columbus returned to Europe from the Caribbean in 1493, he carried with him, among other things, a number of food items including chile peppers, which were quickly embraced by Western European cooks and incorporated into a number of different dishes. From there, peppers diffused into Eastern Europe, Asia, and Indonesia where today they have become important and popular ingredients in a vast number of wonderful dishes.

The process of diffusion is sometimes accompanied by a reverse phenomenon. In recent years, varieties of chile peppers grown in New Mexico and California have, in turn, made their way eastward into the Texas chili hearth.

Pinto beans and other kinds of legumes, as well as tomatoes and other occasional ingredients in chili, were also domesticated in Meso-America, eventually diffusing into Texas and the rest of the world. In addition to chile peppers, pinto beans, and tomatoes, the Meso-Americans gave us corn, chocolate, squash, tobacco, and dozens of other important agricultural products.

During the 1880s, the Canary Islanders migrated to San Antonio where, many believe, they were introduced to chile peppers. Finding this new vegetable quite acceptable and rather complementary to many of their dishes, the islanders added them fresh, dried, ground, and in powdered form to their own recipes.

Over the years, chili con carne has evolved, manifesting a variety of incarnations, some of them markedly different from the prototypes derived from the early years in Texas. The first, and still considered by many to be the purest and most essential, recipe contains meat, peppers, garlic, cumin, oregano, and salt. In a relatively short time, this basic guideline has been stretched, padded, modified, ravaged, savaged, and otherwise changed so that chili offers as many variations as there are cultures associated with the human species.

If chili had any kind of formal hearth, a place of origin where it was introduced to the culture, it was most likely in the streets of San Antonio during the early 1880s. The Alamo City was a bustling place in those days, with travelers passing through. The expanding businesses there attracted trade and visitors from states to the north and east. Newcomers arriving in San Antonio became enamored of the chili they sampled and, on returning to Ohio, Illinois, Indiana, New York, and elsewhere, carried with them their appetite for the spicy new dish they enjoyed in Texas. Just as the ingredients, cultures, and styles gave rise to chili in Texas, this same dish became involved in a diffusion process that saw it introduced into new geographic areas where there resided many different cultures. As a result of a growing demand, restaurants and cafés in the Midwest, Northeast, and even the South began featuring chili on their menus. The farther a traveler ventured from central Texas, however, the greater the differences in this special dish.

One man who became instrumental in enhancing the popularity of chili and therefore aiding in its geographic diffusion was the late humorist Will Rogers. While performing on Broadway and elsewhere, Rogers extolled the virtues of chili so that his audiences felt compelled to sample it. Single-handedly, he created a demand for chili wherever he traveled. Other personalities who followed Rogers, such as the late president of the United States, Texan Lyndon B. Johnson, were also instrumental in diffusing chili out of Texas to the North, East, and South. Before long, chili was being served in fine restaurants in Chicago and New York, and soon it became fashionable among the social elite from Washington, D.C., to Los Angeles, California, to dine out on chili.

As chili was gaining a foothold in far-flung locations miles from the Texas hearth, it continued to undergo changes. Not everyone was comfortable with the pepper-generated "heat" associated with much of the Texas chili. People whose palates were less accepting of the spicy flavor of Texas chili began experimenting, and in a short time, regional preferences took control and cultural dictates intruded upon the basic chili recipe. The result was a strikingly rapid evolution into thousands of different recipes, each manifesting certain regional flavors and characteristics.

Southerners, for the most part those good folks found below the Mason-Dixon Line and essentially east of the Texas and Oklahoma Cross Timbers region, enthusiastically embraced chili con carne and wasted no time at all adapting it to their own culinary styles. As chili made its way into and throughout the American South, some dramatic modifications ensued. With the exception of the Cajuns of Louisiana, Southerners have traditionally manifested a rather low tolerance for hot and spicy foods, so the basic Texas-style chili was softened and rounded by exchanging the flavorful and pungent chiles for the milder bell peppers. When chili powder was used at all, which was rarely, quantities were limited.

History does not record the first addition of beans to chili, but the general consensus is that this practice, eschewed by purists, got its start in the South. Since meat was often hard to come by in the poor Southern states, beans were often added to the chili to stretch it. Over time, beans became a standard ingredient in Southern-style chili. Chili containing beans is apparently preferred throughout most of the Midwest as well as in the Western states such as Colorado and Wyoming. Since much of these two traditionally Western states contain a high percentage of Midwestern migrants, this should come as no surprise. Some take the position that the Midwest was the inspiration for the addition of beans to chili, but most of the blame, however, has been attributed to the South. During the 1950s, Southern agriculture became mechanized, rendering tens of thousands of residents jobless. At the same time, employment opportunities surged throughout Illinois, Indiana, and Ohio as a result of the growing automotive and steel industries, prompting a migration of job-seekers from the South. As normally happens when people migrate, they carry with them their way of life—including religious preferences; their manner of speaking; and their music, drinking, and food preferences.

To satisfy Southern tastes, sugar became a common ingredient in their chili. Among collections of chili recipes, the ones that come out of the South more often than not call for sugar and beans. This comes as no surprise to food historians, for Southerners commonly add sugar to all kinds of dishes, including meats and pots of beans and greens. It wasn't much of a stretch, therefore, when the Dixielanders dumped sugar into chili.

Regardless of where the practice of adding beans to chili originated, chili scholars accept that it is far more common in the American South, the Midwest, and the East than in Texas and the Southwest. Experts who study such things acknowledge what geographers call the "Bean Line," a more or less formalized division between the prominent no-beaners of most of the West and the beaners from the East. To the west of the Bean Line, however, can be found islands of exception in places such as Colorado and Wyoming.

Chili experts tend to agree that beans were initially added as a filler or, in some cases, to serve as a substitute for meat in meat-deprived regions. As time went by, however, Southerners, and others, not only became accustomed to having beans in their chili but also actually liked them. As a result, beans remain a common—and to some, an important—ingredient in some kinds of chili.

Differences in the meat used in chili are also apparent in the South, East, and Midwest. In these regions, the traditional cubed beef or coarsely ground beef called "chili grind" gave way to hamburger, most likely as a result of expediency. Beef was never as plentiful in the South as it was in Texas, and the beef that could be obtained during the early part of the 1900s was often tough, stringy, and tasteless. To render the tough beef edible, residents resorted to grinding it into hamburger.

Though no one knows for certain, many believe that tomatoes were first added to chili in Texas as a result of experimentation. The practice of topping a bowl of chili with a dollop of sour cream has also been attributed to Southerners, though the Midwest has some proponents for this interesting approach as well. As with sugar and beans, Southern recipes for chili con carne often call for sour cream as an ingredient.

The Southern state of Louisiana offers a somewhat spicier chili than most of its Confederate neighbors. Here, the Cajun cooks often substitute or add zesty homemade sausage along with locally grown hot peppers and hot pepper sauces.

Midwestern cultures offer some interesting variations on the basic chili recipe. In locations such as Illinois, Indiana, and Ohio, chili without beans is seldom found, and the meat is generally hamburger as opposed to diced or cubed beef. Although pinto beans are occasionally encountered, kidney beans, great northern beans, and even lima beans are just as likely to be found. Chili purists, of course, would regard the addition of any kind of beans the ultimate blasphemy, and lima beans are indeed a puzzling choice. Such practices, however, are the products of differences in culture and geography.

Near the western edge of the Midwest in Kansas City, Missouri, an odd variation has been factored into the culture of chili. Here, chili con carne can be found served over a bed of macaroni and called "chili-mac." This meal has somehow found its way into the lunch programs of some of the state's public schools. In years past, Kansas City, Missouri, and its counterpart in Kansas were once considered towns where a visitor could often find a good chili parlor.

Located on the north bank of the Ohio River, Cincinnati is a large and important town in Ohio. In recent years, Cincinnati has been referring to itself as "the Chili Capital of the World." Indeed, some literature states that the city of Cincinnati claims more chili parlors per capita than any other burg in the United States. The Cincinnati telephone book lists about one hundred chili parlors in this town of some 370,000 souls, three times more than McDonald's!

Although Texans and other chili purists may not agree with or even like that claim, the fact remains that Cincinnati does a booming chili business. Serious chili eaters, however, would likely not recognize what Cincinnatians call chili, and one principal reason, as explained by the residents, is that the version served here was modified by the contributions of Greek immigrants.

Recipes gleaned from the fine city of Cincinnati reveal ingredients as nontraditional and diverse as cinnamon, allspice, chocolate, and barbeque sauce. Another custom in this southern Ohio town is to pour the mix they call chili over a large helping of spaghetti.

According to purveyors of Cincinnati chili, the most popular version is called the "Five Way" and consists of a large plate of spaghetti topped with a sauce made from hamburger and a number of standard chili seasonings, along with cinnamon, cardamom, turmeric, allspice, chocolate, and barbeque sauce from a jar. Heaped atop this concoction is a large serving of kidney beans that, in turn, is covered by chopped raw onions. Finally, a sprinkling of grated cheddar cheese is added and allowed to melt. Sometimes, this Cincinnati chili is topped with shredded lettuce. The Five Way is customarily served with oyster crackers.

Cincinnatians can also order a Four Way, which comes without onions. Or they may select a Three Way, which arrives sans onions and beans. The Three Way is also called a Haywagon. Another variety is called the Chili Bean, which is basically the Five Way served without cheese and onions.

According to Cincinnati history, these somewhat odd geographic versions of chili were concocted by two brothers from Greece who migrated to the Ohio town in the early 1920s and opened a tiny café. Their credentials for operating an eatery were related to the fact that they ran a hot dog stand in New York City for a couple of years. The brothers, John and Athanas Kiradjieff, experimented with a variety of ingredients and eventually arrived at an early version of Five Way chili, apparently to the delight of Cincinnati natives. So popular was the Kiradjieff's "chili" that dozens of other cafés opened during the next few years featuring the same dish.

Moving northward from the Midwest into the Great Lakes states of Michigan, Minnesota, and Wisconsin, chili lovers find variations that have much in common with their neighbors in Illinois and Indiana. Beans are ubiquitous in Great Lakes chili. According to some recipes gleaned from this area, many of these folks apparently believe chili con carne is supposed to contain more beans than meat. The beans come from cans, and kidneys are the most common.

Some Wisconsin chilis contained, instead of kidney beans, such varieties as red beans and lima beans, but never pinto beans. Rather than fresh, dried, or powdered chiles, bottled salsas were commonly used. Lots of garlic was evident, and the meat was always hamburger.

A number of recipes filed under the heading of "Minnesota chili" reveal ingredients and techniques for preparing a hearty chili-like stew, sometimes substituting wild game for beef. Although some of these recipes resemble others encountered in the Midwest, a few are quite innovative and include ingredients such as apple cider vinegar and wine. Beans are plentiful and are most often kidney.

The industrialized and economically active Northeast is home to tens of thousands of expatriate Texans who drifted into the cooler and more densely populated climes to pursue their fortunes. As a result, the demand in places such as New York and Boston for authentic barbeque, chicken-fried steaks, and Texas chili remains high. Restaurant operators in this part of the country responded by opening a number of barbeque joints and chili parlor–style cafés. Although you can find chili in New York that possesses definite Midwestern characteristics, there also happens to be a lot of traditional Texas-style chili. Recipes obtained from several of these New York outlets verify this observation.

You can also find an acceptable bowl of authentic chili in the nation's capital. The tenure of the late President Lyndon B. Johnson in Washington, D.C., led to some level of popularization of chili here. To this day, you can still find authentic chili at a number of D.C. establishments, though if you are not careful, you could be handed a bowl containing beans, usually kidney.

Just to the west of Texas in the great state of New Mexico, chili con carne is gradually taking on a high-profile identity. Flavorful New Mexico chile peppers—and they are grown in enormous quantities here—contribute some robust and exciting flavors to chili. Here in the Land of Enchantment, pork is commonly added to beef in chili, and in some recipes it replaces the beef altogether. The results, though somewhat nontraditional, are delicious. Where beans are used at all in New Mexico, garbanzos have occasionally been employed with tasteful effect. A number of New Mexico–based recipes also call for corn or hominy, each of which offers a flavor that nicely complements the taste of the pork.

Like New Mexico, California is also making a name for itself from the standpoint of chile pepper agriculture, with Anaheim peppers being the most prominent. In spite of this magnificent resource, a lot of California-style chili recipes served up in the bigger cities use bell peppers instead of chile peppers. Long touted as California's finest chili con carne, the recipe found at Chasen's restaurant in Beverly Hills used green bell peppers instead of real chiles.

For California Five Way Chili, the approach is similar to Cincinnati's Five Way in that it involves layering chili-like stew, beans, onions, and cheese atop a bed of spaghetti. The principal differences are in the ingredients. Spicy Mexican chorizo sausage is added to the hamburger, and considerably more chili powder will be found than in Cincinnati, where it is often absent. In addition, black beans are used instead of kidney beans.

The growing popularity of chili across the country has naturally led to competition. It is estimated that hundreds of chili cook-offs occur in the United States each year, most of them sanctioned by the International Chili Society (ICS) or the Chili Appreciation Society International (CASI). Chili cook-offs, like chili itself, have grown to become cultural institutions as well as an art form, complete with costumes, displays, and even live music.

The Chili Appreciation Society International and the International Chili Society oversee most of the chili competition in the United States and elsewhere and are responsible for keeping track of chili activity throughout this country as well as others. Members of these two organizations come from practically every state in the union. Not only do these two fine groups sponsor and sanction chili cook-offs, they also offer an opportunity for kindred spirits and fellow chilimeisters to gather and interact at a wide variety of locations.

The CASI championship chili cook-off was the reigning chili event in the world between 1967 and 1974, held in the remote West Texas town of Terlingua. This competition still attracts huge crowds and fierce competition.

Due to differences in philosophy, Carol Shelby and C. V. Wood broke away from CASI to help form the ICS and established headquarters in Newport Beach, California. One of the first tasks of the new ICS was to establish its own world championship cook-off, which was accomplished with great success. For years, the ICS world championships were held in California, but in 1996, the event was moved to Las Vegas, Nevada.

CASI boasts "chili pods" in about twenty-four U.S. states as well as several foreign countries. Each of these pods may hold a local cook-off. Over four hundred CASI-sponsored events are held each year and operate according to very strict rules. Chili is judged on the basis of aroma, color, taste, aftertaste, and texture. Because only true and authentic chili qualifies, beans are strictly forbidden. Points are awarded to cooks who place in the top ten at CASI-sanctioned cook-offs, and after receiving a certain critical number, cooks can qualify for the annual national cook-off at Terlingua.

The ICS is a nonprofit organization that sanctions chili cook-offs with specific rules for judging and cooking. Their stated purpose is, in part, "to promote, develop, and improve the preparation and appreciation of true chili and to determine each year the World's Champion Chili through officially sanctioned and regulated competitive cook-offs."

The ICS championship cook-off may likely be the world's largest food contest. During a recent ICS world championship cook-off elimination, more than 9,000 cooks from around the country participated. The 250 finalists at Las Vegas competed for $40,000 in prize money, and more than 25,000 visitors attended the events.

Both the CASI and ICS are active in community service and raise money for charities. The CASI has contributed more than three quarters of a million dollars to charities over the years. According to the ICS web page, about $65,000,000 has been raised by charities holding sanctioned cook-offs.

Sanctioned chili cook-offs require entries of authentic and near-authentic chili only. It must be cooked from scratch, beginning with raw, unmarinated meat. Commercial chili powder is allowed, but chili mixes—blends of chili powder and other spices and herbs—are not permitted. Also not allowed in competition chili is the addition of beans, macaroni, rice, hominy, or any other fillers.

Throughout the United States, indeed, the world, there exist uncountable varieties of the dish known as chili con carne. The variations have come about as a result of differences in available ingredients, local tastes, and cultural tolerances and desires for certain kinds of foods. The enormous success of chili and its widespread diffusion testify to its satisfying nature. Having become adapted to innumerable and quite diverse cultures, chili has remained a popular food and an important business, one having significant economic impact throughout a wide region.

# THREE
# fixins

Cool autumn evenings cause my thoughts to turn to killin' a hog, cuttin' firewood, and cookin' up a big pot o' chili.

—Anonymous

When you enter and explore the ranks of America's chili cooks, you discover a myriad of choices, options, and sometimes even confusion about the "fixins," essentially a Texas word that refers to the chili ingredients, condiments, and accompaniments. Fixins are also referred to as "makins" in some parts of the country.

The quality of your chili will depend, clearly, on what you put into it. In addition to the attitude, emotion, and love you invest in a good pot of chili, the actual fixins you include can make or break your reputation as a chili cook. The right fixins, prepared with care, can elevate an average chili cook to one with distinction and honor. Poor and inadequate fixins can not only ruin a pot of chili quicker than a rain shower can ruin a picnic but can also ruin reputations and make pariahs out of otherwise good folks.

Fixins include meat, peppers, other vegetables, spices, toppings, sides, and even liquids. To some people, fixins can mean beans.

## meat

Let's get one thing clear: Chili is a meat and chile pepper dish, always has been, period. *Carne* is the Spanish word for meat. Meat and ground, powdered, or chopped chiles represent the major ingredients in traditional chili, both in quantity and for determining taste.

Virtually any kind of meat can be used in the preparation of chili, but beef is the most common and most preferred. Cheap, tough cuts of meat were originally used for chili. Joe Cooper always insisted that chili should be made with mature beef, but practiced chili cooks are able to concoct an excellent pot of chili with cheaper cuts of meat. Many have experimented with and arrived at some fine pots of chili using meat from armadillo, rattlesnake, venison, pork, elk, antelope, rabbit, turkey, chicken, fish, and even opossum, crow, and horse. There are even reports of some good pots of chili made from kangaroo meat! During the 1960s while working on a ranch in West Texas, I had some chili made from bull testicles, and frankly, it was darned tasty. On the other hand, I have learned from experience that veal makes a poor chili.

Regardless of your particular meat preferences, the first choice of professional chili cooks is beef, and beef is what is generally encountered in sanctioned chili cook-offs. While virtually all kinds, cuts, and grades of beef have been used in making chili, lean is preferred. Sirloin and sirloin tip appear to be more favored than any other cut, and dozens of prize-winning recipes call for them. A nice arm, blade, or shoulder roast, chopped or ground appropriately, can also yield some spectacular results.

Acceptable chili can be made from less expensive cuts such as round steak, and if you are on a budget, such cuts prove quite satisfactory. Avoid cheap, fatty cuts and gristle.

A lot of people around the country who make chili at home have been led to believe that good chili can be made from hamburger. Depending on whom you are feeding, you might get by on hamburger, but it is considered a poor substitute by the experienced. Serious chili cooks regard people who use ground beef as Philistines. Cooper once wrote, "Only barbarians and Yankees make chili with ground meat."

According to my research and experience, most who employ hamburger in the making of chili are found in the American South and the Midwest, and to a lesser extent in the Northeast. Given what some of these folks do to chili, however, the use of hamburger is among the least of their sins.

Chili experts are in agreement that the lean meat used should be cubed, not ground. Cubes should be no more than one-half inch square, perhaps slightly smaller. Several chili cooks I know prefer quarter-inch cubes. You can easily cube the meat with a sharp knife or have your butcher do it. Usually, there is no extra charge at good meat markets. If using other meats besides beef, you should also cube them. Some parts of a chicken as well as rattlesnake are not easily cubed, so do the best you can.

If you do not care for cubed meat, the next best thing is coarse-grinding. Many butcher shops and supermarkets throughout Texas and the American Southwest commonly offer what is called "chili grind," a coarsely ground lean beef ideal for making chili. Do not confuse chili grind with hamburger. In chili grind, the individual pieces of meat are larger than those found in hamburger and somewhat smaller than the cubes but wind up being quite satisfactory. My experience has indicated that chili grind is virtually unknown and largely unavailable outside of the Southwest.

# chile peppers

If beef is the heart of chili, the chile peppers are the soul. When peppers are used in the making of chili, the cook is faced with an embarrassment of riches, for there is a wide and flavorful variety from which to choose. Many cooks have their favorites and employ them over and over. Others vary the kinds of chile peppers in order to provide different tastes. Experimenting with different kinds of chiles is fun, enlightening, and adventurous. It can't hurt you and does not break any rules. The processes of experimenting and discovering are important in cooking and can lead to some satisfying results.

Technically, chiles are not peppers according to strict food classifications. Bell peppers are true peppers. The confusion arose when Christopher Columbus encountered the hot and spicy chiles in the Caribbean Islands. He misidentified them as peppers, and the term "chile peppers" has been used ever since. The early Spanish conquistadores added somewhat to the confusion. When they arrived among the Incas and tasted some of the food prepared for them, they believed the strong spice they encountered came from a kind of black pepper they were used to back home. Thereafter, the Spaniards, like Columbus, referred to them as chile peppers.

Though different varieties of peppers are now grown around the world, most chiles are uniquely Meso-American in origin. Happily, several regional cuisines have benefited from the more than two hundred or so chile peppers known to exist.

The so-called heat associated with hot peppers comes from the veins and membranes in the pod and not from the seeds as so many people believe. As a general rule, the more pointed the chile, the hotter it is. Likewise, on the average, the smaller the chile, the hotter it tends to be. The habanero pepper, a rounded, orange-colored chile just a little bigger than a large grape is among the hottest of the world's chiles. When you are preparing peppers for chili, whether fresh or dried, the stems, seeds, and peels are normally removed and discarded.

Chile peppers, first and foremost, provide flavor for chili con carne. The heat is merely a by-product, although many mistakenly believe chili is not authentic unless it is hot. The heat, to be sure, can add a dimension to chili but should never be done at the expense of flavor. The active ingredient in chile peppers that provides the heat is an alkaloid named capsaicin, and the genus to which chiles belong is Capsicum.

The peppers used in making chili can be found in most good supermarkets and specialty stores. They can be found fresh, dried, ground, powdered, canned, or, rarely, in paste form. There are many varieties to select from to satisfy the most adventurous and experimental cooks and those with low tolerance for hot and spicy peppers. For the meek, bell peppers can be used. Chili powder, made from powdered chile along with other ingredients, is such an important element to any chili recipe that it will be treated separately later in this chapter.

When using fresh peppers, dice or chop and sauté the peppers early during preparation, depending on the recipe. Some prefer to puree them. Normally, the peppers can be sautéed along with the onions and garlic.

For those who like a hotter, more robust chili, additional diced fresh chile peppers are sometimes added during the simmering that takes place at the end of the recipe. They can simply be tossed into the pot and stirred into the contents or added as a topping when served, as is done in many chili parlors. The amount can be adjusted to suit your tastes or those of your fellow diners.

Before using fresh chile peppers, make certain they are peeled. This is always a bit of added trouble, but if you don't do this, the skins will work loose during the cooking process, and they are not particularly desirable from a texture stand-point and are not digestible.

Some like to roast their chiles before adding them to the pot. Roasting adds flavor, and once roasted, the skin can easily be peeled off. Roasting can be done on a barbeque grill or in an oven turned up to around 400 degrees. When the skins on the peppers begin to blister, remove them from the heat and peel.

When handling chile peppers, particularly the very hot ones like habaneros and some jalapenos, refrain from rubbing the eyes or genital area. Some who have a low tolerance for the external effects of the capsaicin sometimes suffer su-perficial but nevertheless annoyingly painful burns that can last for hours. Some who handle chile peppers while cooking suggest that buttering the hands and fin-gers keeps them safe from the burning effects of the capsaicin. I have found this to be minimally effective and have taken to wearing thin, disposable rubber gloves while handling extremely hot chile peppers. Should you experience a burn, treat the affected area with a paste made from baking soda and water, a commercial salve, or a fresh slice of aloe vera. Should you experience a burn in your mouth from a hot chile pepper, take a mouthful of water and hold it for several minutes to cool the affected area, spit it out, then drink some milk.

Here are a few chile peppers worth considering in the preparation of chili con carne:

## anaheim

The Anaheim, also called the California chile, is a green chile that can grow to a length of approximately seven inches. The Anaheim has a pleasant, mild taste and, while a favorite for many, is considered too tame for those who like their chili really hot. When used in chili con carne, the Anaheim is often accompanied by other hotter chiles. When dried, the Anaheim takes on a deep reddish color. You can usually find fresh Anaheims in the produce section of any good supermarket. They can also be found canned and are often labeled "green chiles."

## ancho

Ancho is a Spanish term for *wide*, and indeed these tasty peppers are wide near the stem, tapering toward the end and forming a kind of long triangle. Anchos are the dried versions of poblanos, wide pods around four inches long. The poblano, if not dried and used in chili as an ancho, is a favorite ingredient in a number of delicious pork stews. The ancho can range from dark red to almost black in color. As chiles go, anchos are not particularly hot for most diners but are very delicious. They are generally the favored pepper for chili con carne, being just slightly hotter than the popular Anaheim and, according to some, considerably tastier. In California and along the west coast of Mexico, the ancho is called the pasilla. This is sometimes confusing, since a true pasilla pepper is a relatively narrow, six-inch-long, brownish chile pepper.

## arbol

Powdered chile arbol can often be found in specialty stores and is a favored ingredient in chili among a number of devoted cook-off competitors. The arbol, a close relative of the cayenne, grows to about three inches in length and when mature is a fiery red in color. This somewhat hot chile also offers a delicious taste and provides a bit of fire to your pot of chili. The arbol is not for sissies.

## cayenne

The cayenne is a common ingredient in many chili recipes, usually added in the powdered form. This thin, red pepper, between four and seven inches long, tends to be hot but quite flavorful. The cayenne has become extremely popular in parts of Asia and is used extensively in a variety of cuisines.

## chipotle

See jalapeno.

## guajillo

The guajillo pepper is occasionally found in Mexican specialty food stores and is usually labeled "mirasol." It is an orange-red to brown pepper, tapered, about five inches long and one-and-a-half inches wide. The guajillo has a sweeter taste than most chiles.

## habanero

The habanero pepper, looking deceptively like a miniature, shriveled bell pepper, has a reputation as one of the two hottest chiles in the world. Long used in cooking in Mexico, the habanero has grown in popularity in the United States in recent years so that it is now sometimes found in the fresh produce sections of good supermarkets. Small amounts of habanero pepper are often used in Texas-style barbeque sauces. If you are compelled to add habanero peppers to your chili, be aware that a little bit goes a long, long way. Only a few hardy and tough-throated cooks regularly use them in chili these days.

## jalapeno

Due to the growing popularity of Tex-Mex cuisine around the country, even the world, the jalapeno has become a rather ubiquitous chile. One reason for its popularity is that it is darned tasty, though somewhat hot for those with sensitive palates. Long common in Texas and the Southwest, jalapenos can be found in grocery stores as far north as Montana, and a friend who lives in Connecticut happily reported he found fresh jalapenos in his supermarket in Hartford.

Jalapenos grow to about three inches long and are normally picked when they are green. Left to ripen on the plant, they will turn red. They can be purchased fresh, canned, and frozen. Fresh is always best, but if not available, the other types are not bad. For those who like their chili hot and also like the flavor of jalapeno peppers, fresh ones are generally chopped or minced and added to the pot during the last half hour of cooking. Dried and crushed jalapenos are not as ubiquitous in stores as are the fresh and canned ones but can be found in specialty shops and mail-order houses.

Also growing in popularity are chipotles, which are dried and smoked jalapenos. Chipotles added to chili con carne provide not only the heat desired by many but also a rich, smoky flavor unlike any other pepper.

## New Mexico
The New Mexico chile has been described as a hybrid and is fast becoming popular with chili cooks around the country. Closely related to an Anaheim and similar in appearance, the New Mexico chile offers rich, robust flavor with a significant amount of heat. New Mexico chiles come in green and red and can be found fresh, dried, frozen, and powdered.

## pasilla
A more common name for the pasilla is the *chile negro* because of its dark, almost black color. Looking much like an Anaheim, the pasilla is fairly spicy and hot, smells a bit like raisins, and is considered by a number of chiliheads as a serious and important pepper. Pasilla is commonly used as an ingredient in chili powders.

## pequin
Chile pequins are tiny, almost the size and shape of raisins, and often found growing wild along the Texas–Mexico border. Some chili historians believe that the pequin may have been the first chile pepper used in making chili for the

cowhands during the early trail drive days through Texas. They are still favored by those who like their chili good and hot. In fact, a number of chili purists claim that any chili made without pequins is not authentic.

## poblano
See ancho.

## scotch bonnet
This little chile pepper looks a lot like a habanero and is just about as hot. Although occasionally used in chile recipes, the scotch bonnet is not particularly common in the United States and offers no substantial improvement over the more common habanero.

## serrano
Serrano chiles have also been growing in popularity lately among those who like a hot pepper in their chili con carne. This rather thin, two-inch-long chile is a bit hotter than a jalapeno and has found many fans among those who like a hot pot of chili. Serranos, like a few other types of chiles, can be found pickled and for sale in a variety of supermarkets. Though hot, they are quite flavorful.

# onions
Regardless of how you may feel about onions, many chili cooks are convinced you cannot make real chili without them. Some, however, eschew them altogether. Ultimately, personal tastes and preferences should be your guide here. As with chile peppers, a wide variety of onions is available.

Following years of observation, I believe that yellow onions are the most commonly preferred in the making of chili. This seems appropriate, since yellow onions are plentiful, tasty, and inexpensive.

Some prefer purple or red onions. Purples and reds offer a somewhat different flavor than yellows and work rather well in chili. Purples and reds tend to be more expensive than yellows but not prohibitively so.

A few chiliheads prefer a sweeter tasting onion such as a Vidalia. Available in most fine grocery stores, Vidalias have a great flavor and can make a wonderful contribution to a pot of chili.

I have also dined on chili made with green onions, leeks, and scallions. While I didn't find them in the least bit objectionable, they lack the punch and flavor of a good yellow onion.

The size of the chopped pieces of onion varies among chili cooks. Some prefer to dice the onions real fine, almost minced, prior to sautéing. This, they claim, enables the tiny pieces practically to dissolve in the pot. Others, and I am among them, prefer the onion chopped into pieces roughly the size of your smallest fingernail before sautéing. Some of us care little about having our onions disappear into the liquid, preferring instead to experience the direct taste and texture of this wonderful and versatile vegetable.

# tomatoes

Discussion of tomatoes as an ingredient in authentic chili can be a dangerous undertaking. Strict traditionalists rarely employ tomatoes in the preparation of chili con carne and reject any bowl of red containing that particular fruit. World renowned chilisto Joe Cooper once quoted E. DeGolyer as saying that the use of tomatoes in chili, ripe or canned, was regarded as "effeminate." Though some will disagree with him, Cooper further claimed that the presence of tomato in chili detracts from the flavor provided by the chile pepper.

Whether or not you believe in the use of tomatoes in chili, the fact remains, however unpleasant it may be for some, that a number of world champion recipes employ them as an ingredient and sometimes as a topping or garnish. A number of such recipes are included in this book.

Some claim they add tomatoes for flavor, others argue they are for color, and still others maintain they use them for texture and liquid. A few who do not use tomatoes during the actual cooking of the chili con carne sometimes apply fresh chopped tomatoes as a garnish.

For those who like to use tomatoes, fresh is best. Some claim they will add only fresh, homegrown tomatoes, taking the position that the store-bought fruit is tasteless. Unfortunately, many who do not have their own gardens are forced to purchase tomatoes in the supermarkets. Supermarket tomatoes, on the whole, tend to be a rather unsatisfactory product for cooks searching for full flavor. Most tomatoes found in grocery stores are hydroponically grown. They are essentially laboratory tomatoes nurtured in a liquid slurry of fertilizer that circulates beneath a rack that holds the fruit. The roots of these poor little tomato plants never touch soil, a source of flavor and nutrition. As a result, supermarket tomatoes have the taste and personality of a piece of cardboard. You would be just as well off to purchase canned tomatoes if the garden variety is not available.

If you use fresh tomatoes in your recipe, make certain you peel them beforehand. Tomato peels in a pot of chili are as unwanted and unloved as chile peels. One advantage of using the canned tomatoes is that they are already peeled.

Tomatoes, canned or fresh, are often added to chili for the liquid. Some will use tomato sauce, while others prefer tomato juice. Spicy tomato juice cocktail has been employed to good effect. A caution is required here. If you are a tomato user, be careful not to overdo it. Too much tomato can ruin the flavor of an otherwise good pot of chili.

Another word of caution: Over the years I have discovered that a few misguided souls substitute catsup for tomato in their chili recipes. Catsup offers few, if any, positives for a bowl of chili but adds a host of negatives, mostly undesirable ingredients such as sugar and preservatives.

# other vegetables

More and more chili recipes today contain additional vegetables such as celery, carrots, corn, bell peppers, and tofu. Depending on what the other ingredients are, these nontraditional newcomers to chili con carne can impart an acceptable and complementary taste. For example, when pork is substituted for beef in certain recipes, the addition of corn or hominy results in a delicious chili-like stew. Most chilis, however, will not suffer from the absence of these vegetables.

Chili purists insist there is no place whatsoever for the likes of celery, carrots, corn, and bell peppers and recommend you refrain from experimenting. Although I remain traditional at heart, my soul calls for the adventure of experimenting as you see fit.

# herbs and spices

Herbs and spices, as they relate to chili con carne, are often misunderstood. It is true that a wide variety of spices and seasonings gets tossed into chili pots around the country, but many of them are not necessary. The secret is not in the number of spices used, but in the blend. Traditionally, the most successful blend of spices, as it relates to chili, consists of salt, red or black pepper, chili powder, cumin, garlic, occasionally oregano, and sometimes paprika. There will be those who would argue with this list, but it results from years of research.

Most who are concerned about the quality of ingredients for the preparation of chili purchase seasonings from supply houses instead of grocery stores. The difference in taste is clear. Furthermore, purchasing seasonings, herbs, and chili powders from a well-established supply house can save a lot of money over time.

Other seasonings have been employed with good results, and I offer an inventory here. In case you need to refer to this list in the future, they are listed in alphabetical order so your search will be made easier.

## basil

Basil, and sometimes sweet basil, is occasionally used in chili. If tomatoes are included in the recipe, basil is recommended since it complements the red fruit. Otherwise, it will hurt nothing if you leave it out.

## bay leaf

A bay leaf or two can be added to your chili without inflicting any harm. While a bay leaf floating on top of a pot of chili might look good to some, I have never been convinced it contributes a single important flavor to the overall taste. If you use a bay leaf, be sure to remove it before serving.

## cilantro

Cilantro and coriander are in great demand these days as a result of the growing popularity of Tex-Mex cuisine. Cilantro is also called Chinese parsley or Mexican parsley. Coriander is the seed of the plant that yields cilantro. Since cilantro adds to the flavor of a wide variety of such cuisines, many believe it will also be suitable for use in chili. I rather like cilantro and have found that a small amount works well in chili, but it depends on how it is used. When serving a bowl of chili, try sprinkling a bit of cilantro on top. The taste is best appreciated in this manner. Cooking the cilantro with the chili is a waste of good seasoning.

## cumin

Next to black pepper, cumin is considered to be the most popular seasoning in the world. No chili cook worth his or her salt would consider preparing a bowl o' red without cumin. It comes powdered and as whole seeds. Here is something I learned a long time ago: If you can get seeds, try roasting them in the oven or searing them in a skillet for several minutes. Then grind them up and add the requisite amount to your chili. The fresher the seeds, the better. They are hard to beat for taste.

## garlic

Without wishing to generate an argument, let me state that garlic, though technically a vegetable, is also an herb. There are several varieties of garlic, ranging from sweet to pungent, and the only rule associated with it is to use the amount you like best.

Professional chili cooks use garlic cloves minced well before sautéing. Some cooks have successfully employed granulated and powdered garlic to enhance the flavor of their chili. The alternatives work well and are easy to use but somehow lack the full-bodied flavor of the fresh cloves. My opinion is that the mincing of at least a couple of fresh garlic cloves is well worth the effort if you are interested in cooking a great pot of chili.

## oregano

Oregano is considered by many to be an essential ingredient for chili. Many chili cooks, including me, purchase oregano in bulk and use it liberally in chili as well as in a variety of sauces and stews. To my way of thinking, however, you must use a lot of oregano in chili con carne in order to taste it. While I regularly use oregano in my recipes, some argue that chili would not suffer if it were left out.

## paprika

Ground paprika is a welcome and desirable ingredient in a lot of chili recipes. Paprika is actually a pepper, and while some like it for the taste it imparts to chili and other dishes, some cooks I know add it for color and a little bit of heat. I prefer Hungarian paprika over the Mexican paprika because it is stronger. If you can find it, try some smoked paprika the next time you cook up a batch of chili. It offers a robust taste that has delighted legions of chili eaters.

## salt

Salt is a necessary ingredient for chili. Salt brings out the true flavor of meat like no other seasoning. If you happen to be on a salt-free diet, you don't need to be eating chili unless you can find a suitable substitute. Most cooks use plain old table salt, but for a slightly more exotic and altogether pleasant taste, try sea salt. It is generally found in health food stores and in a few good supermarkets.

## thyme

Thyme is rarely added to chili, but in the few recipes that call for it, this herb, used sparingly, imparts an interesting and acceptable flavor.

## woodruff

Woodruff is a seasoning found in the recipes of famous chili cooks Woody De-Silva and Ormly Gumfudgin. It is not readily available on grocery store shelves. Gumfudgin informs me that woodruff is the first seasoning mentioned in the Bible. Regardless, only a few chili cooks have ever heard of it, and even fewer use it.

# chili powder

Beginning chili cooks often confuse chili powder with powdered chile. Powdered chile is simply a quantity of a kind of chile, say ancho or Anaheim, that has been finely powdered and sold most often in a plastic envelope-style package. Chili powders include powdered chile but contain other ingredients such as cumin, oregano, and garlic powder. Not all chili powders are the same, and portions of each ingredient may vary from supplier to supplier. Some add salt; some don't.

Traditionally, powdered ancho chiles are most often found in commercial chili powders, but growing interest in chili cooking has led to the use of other types of peppers, such as pasilla. Some adventurous souls even add a half-teaspoon or so of powdered habanero pepper to the mix for some extra zing.

If you are compelled to use the commercial chili powders you find on the supermarket shelves rather than make your own or acquire them from a good supplier, stick with well-known brands. Go with quality. Several lesser-known brands of chili powder tend to be inferior and ultimately lead to an inferior pot of chili.

Some advanced levels of chili cooking often call for powdered chile, not chili powder. Pure powdered chile comes in a number of varieties, including New

Mexico, ancho, Anaheim, California, and pasilla. A few new hybrids are also growing in popularity. The purest of the purists purchase the whole, dried chile pods and grind or puree their own.

The type of chili powder and powdered chile you use is best determined via experimentation, one of my favorite parts of cooking chili.

# sweeteners

When you examine recipes for chili con carne that come out of the American South—south of the Mason-Dixon Line and east of the Mississippi but also including Arkansas—you discover that sugar is a common ingredient. Since authentic chili does not call for sugar, and since most dedicated chili cooks would rather be stabbed than put sugar in their pot, this addition baffled me for years until I discovered the reason. Southern cooks tend to put sugar in everything— chili, soups, beans, greens, stews, and other dishes. It appears to be a cultural habit for many of them, one that is apparently not easily broken. While many would regard adding sugar as a sacrilege, I have heard one or two compelling arguments in favor of it.

Not long ago, I had a conversation with a championship chili cook who admitted that he, and a few others he knew, often added a bit of sugar or other sweetener to the chili pot. This is done, he stated, to round out and subdue what can be harsh or bitter flavors of the chili powder, paprika, and chile peppers. He also showed me a couple of world championship chili recipes that, indeed, called for a small amount of sugar.

For my part, I love, even crave, the unsweetened flavor of chili con carne, of the chili powder, paprika, and peppers, but I also appreciate the notion that some are sensitive to them.

I have tried experimenting with sugars and other sweeteners in the past but over the years ultimately rejected them. If, however, you must add some kind of sweetener, stay away from refined table sugar and use brown sugar. I also tried honey once and found it to yield a pleasant sweetness. A friend once suggested using a tablespoonful of cocoa powder. I tried it, but it was little better than plain sugar.

During the past few years, I've discussed this issue with some who belong to the round-out-the-flavor-and-subdue-the-biting-flavor school of thought but who dislike sugar as much as I do. They have introduced me to other ingredients such as chocolate, cinnamon, molasses, and agave nectar. Ultimately, I prefer a more traditional pot of chili without a sweetener, but if you must add a sweetener in order to enjoy your chili, then it must be done.

# liquids

Since chili is essentially a kind of meat stew, some amount of liquid is required. Some chili cooks simply add water, which works just fine. Many rely on the juice from tomatoes, fresh or canned. Those who need to add liquids but are deeply concerned about unnecessarily diluting the flavor have discovered a number of alternatives.

Beef broth and chicken broth are appearing more regularly in some excellent chili recipes. I have used both beef and chicken broth from time to time, splashing a bit into the cooking pot when fluids get low, and I rather like it. The chicken broth adds a nice flavor to the chili, but you want to be careful not to overdo it.

Several championship chili recipes call for beer, which some believe adds a nice punch. You need not be concerned with the alcohol content of the pot of chili because most of it quickly cooks away. Should you choose to try beer the next time you need to add some liquid, I recommend a dark, hearty Mexican brand such as Dos Equis or Tecate. They are so much more flavorful than the watered-down American beers.

I have dined on chili where some red wine was added for liquid. It was not too bad, but the wine didn't work as well as broth or beer. On the other hand, I sometimes raise the level of the liquid in my chili pot by adding a couple of shots of high-quality tequila. The results are quite tasty. If you choose to add tequila, make certain you use one made with 100% blue agave, not the cheap brands favored by college fraternities. The label on the bottle will state whether or not the tequila is made from pure blue agave. If not stated, the tequila is diluted with approximately 40% cane alcohol. The difference is substantial, especially in chili.

In recent years, I have experienced some chili con carne that included whiskey as a liquid. A half-cup of good whiskey provides a flavor like nothing else and is worth a try.

Some other liquids have been used with success. Surprisingly, a tablespoon or two of vinegar does wonders for a pot of chili, as does a similar amount of lime juice. Some prefer lemon juice, but the taste of lime somehow works better with chili than does the lemon. Work it out among yourselves.

# cooking oil

One of the concessions traditional chili cooks have made in recent years is related to the cooking oil used. Initially, the meat was browned in fat, the favorite being kidney suet. If suet was not available, the meat was cooked in grease from bacon or salt pork or in lard. While fat provides considerably more flavor to chili than cooking oils, growing concerns relative to health and cholesterol have led to the general abandonment of fats during the preparation of chili and have inspired cooks to examine a number of alternatives.

The truth is that the fat accounts for the taste in meat, whether barbequing, broiling, frying, or adding to chili and other stews. A little fat is probably OK, but too much of the saturated kind consumed too often can, according to medical research, lead to heart and other health-related problems. As a result, even the staunchest chiliheads have weaned themselves off of fat and lard and have switched to low-cholesterol cooking oils. After all, you want to be around for a long time to enjoy the pleasures of bowls and bowls of chili.

The cooking oil, of course, is employed in the browning of the meat. By and large, any good cooking oil will do, with extra-virgin olive oil preferred by most.

Canola oil is also seen a lot during chili cook-off competitions. I personally prefer olive oil for health considerations; I heartily recommend it and use it in all of my own recipes. Although many have grown fond of the taste of olive oil, you can employ whatever cooking oil you prefer.

Speaking of oils and fats, a professional and highly successful chili competitor once told me for the best results, use goose fat for browning the meat. This fat, he claims, brings out the flavor of the meat like no other. Goose fat, however, does not stack up against olive oil and canola oil as far as health considerations go, and it is also not easily obtained.

# thickenings

The use of thickenings in chili has provoked an argument or two over the past few decades. Some, who claim to be purists, simply never use thickening and maintain that no decent, authentic pot of chili requires a thickening agent. Others argue that adding some thickening provides an acceptable texture to chili con carne.

I care little for thickenings, though I confess to having dined occasionally on chili that contained some. Thickenings, most chili enthusiasts would agree, are part of the ruination of canned chili. Thickenings used in large quantities can detract from a good bowl of chili.

If you are inclined to add a thickening, try masa harina, a finely ground cornmeal. Masa is easily obtained in supermarkets throughout the Southwest and generally encountered in specialty food stores in some parts of the rest of the country. Soak a little masa overnight in some water until you achieve the consistency of a viscous paste. Squeeze a bit of lime juice into it and mix well for some added flavor. The next day, during the final cooking phase of your pot of chili con carne, add just a little bit of the masa paste at a time to the mix until you have achieved the consistency you require.

If you are unable to acquire masa harina, flour tends to be the alternative of choice. Some soak the flour overnight, others just add a couple of tablespoons right out of the bag to the pot of chili. Other thickeners I have encountered in the past include coarse-ground cornmeal, cracker meal, and even oatmeal, which is used a lot in canned chilis as a thickener and a stretcher.

# beans

A touchy subject, beans in chili have been argued and fought about for decades. Those who are committed to cooking traditional authentic chili may skip this section. Legitimate, sanctioned chili con carne competitions strictly forbid the use of beans, but many citizens of this country claim to enjoy a bowl of chili with beans added.

There is scant evidence relative to the first use of beans in chili, but most who study such things suggest it was associated with the necessity to stretch the food supply during lean times, added when there was not much meat to be had. The use of beans, according to the available literature on the subject, appears to be most common in the Midwest and the South, and considerably less so in Texas and the Southwest.

Beans served in a small bowl alongside a bowl of chili is quite traditional and even expected at some tables. If you have friends over for a chili supper, arrivals who expect beans in their chili are completely at liberty to scoop them into their bowls while others turn their heads.

Beans cooked into the chili, however, become another matter. To many committed chili cooks, placing beans in the concoction invites comparisons from the knowledgeable and risks scorn from the chili elite. Reputations have been destroyed as a result of such culinary *faux pas*, social standings have plummeted, and otherwise good people have become the butt of cruel jokes. If, however, you continue to insist on using beans in chili con carne, here are a few pointers.

If you must add beans to chili, your first choice should be the traditional and tasty pinto bean. The pinto, a tasty bean in its own right, is most likely the favorite of the bean-adders.

Kidney beans are often used in the making of chili con carne with beans, and I have heard testimony from dozens of Northerners and Easterners that kidneys taste very good in a bowl o' red and they wouldn't have it any other way. I have eaten some excellent homemade chili containing kidney beans, and I didn't die from it. Kidney beans also tend to be a touch sweeter than pinto beans.

Red beans have also been used. In fact, some rather tasty chili I've sampled in Cajun Louisiana included red beans in the recipe. Reds, like kidneys, tend to be somewhat sweeter than the pintos.

I love great northern beans and often prepare them at home. While I have encountered great northern beans in chili in the great North such as in Wisconsin, Minnesota, and Michigan, I am convinced it is a poor use of this wonderful legume.

While traveling throughout the American South, I have encountered chili con carne made with butter beans and even black-eyed peas! Once in Arkansas, I was served a bowl of chili that was made with canned pork and beans. It was a horrible experience. In the American Midwest, lima beans and navy beans have been added to chili.

While canned beans are handy and easy, cooking your own beans from a quantity of dried ones is best. Soak the pinto beans, or the kidneys, or reds, or whatever, overnight and cook them the next day the way you like them. Canned beans tend to be slightly mushier and often contain preservatives and other ingredients you may not want in your recipe.

# toppings and accompaniments

If made correctly, a good bowl of chili doesn't need anything else. Some, however, prefer to top their chili with one or more items and serve some extras on the side. Garnishes can add color as well as flavor, and a plate of some kind of bread nearby can complement the chili. Here are some examples of garnishes and accompaniments.

## avocado

Some like to slice an avocado thinly and lay the pieces atop the bowl of chili. The avocado adds a nice green color but, quite frankly, is not complementary to the other tastes found in a bowl o' red.

## catsup

I have occasionally witnessed someone dining on chili con carne in a restaurant dumping catsup into the bowl. Only someone who has not been exposed to the joys of authentic chili would consider doing such a thing. Some canned and commercial chilis are so bad that a dollop or two of catsup might actually improve them, but that is hard to imagine.

## cheese

I have occasionally been served a bowl of chili con carne with shredded cheese sprinkled across the surface. I have observed people apply shredded Swiss, cheddar, Monterey jack, mozzarella, feta, and even parmesan. I love chili and I love cheese, but I rarely mix the two. If the chili is made correctly, the addition of cheese can actually detract from the flavor. On the other hand, if the chili is bad, the addition of cheese may help a little.

## chile peppers

Fresh, chopped chiles, such as jalapenos or serranos, are sometimes added as a garnish and introduced to spice up the chili. Some like to add chopped peppers for color. Chile pequins have been used if the effect desired was to increase the heat content. Poblanos and Anaheims sliced lengthwise and laid across the top of the bowl can also be good.

## cilantro

Tiny amounts of cilantro are sometimes included in chili recipes, but the flavor is essentially camouflaged by other ingredients. Fresh cilantro, chopped and applied as a garnish atop a bowl o' red, can often be quite tasty.

## corn bread

Corn bread is one of the most popular accompaniments to chili con carne. There is something about cornmeal that enhances the taste of chili. Sliced, buttered corn bread as a side is hard to beat. Some like to crumble their corn bread into the chili much as others do with crackers.

## crackers

Saltine crackers are a common accompaniment to chili con carne. Some diners like to crumble their crackers onto the top of their chili, a kind of saltine garnish. Others prefer to stir the crumbles into the chili, a sort of last-minute and unnecessary filler. Crackers, I have been told, were initially served with chili to absorb grease, but over the years diners developed a taste for them. Crackers are also commonly eaten as a side instead of bread or corn bread.

## drinks

What you select to drink with your chili should be purely a matter of personal preference, and there is little agreement among chiliheads as to which is the best. Because dairy products help ease the burn from hot chile peppers, many prefer milk, and some I know cannot eat a bowl of chili without a big glass of cold, sweet milk nearby. I know a man who claims buttermilk is even better. Iced tea is commonly consumed with chili but lacks the soothing effect of milk. Iced water is the choice of many, and beer and hard liquor also have their adherents.

## fritos and other chips

I suppose inevitably two foods that had their origins in Texas would combine into one. Some folks like to add Fritos and other types of corn chips to their chili instead of crackers.

## olives

Once in a while I encounter a bowl of chili garnished with ripe or green olives. This has occurred mostly in the northern part of the country. In a few other experiences, I have found olives added as a chili ingredient. After several tries, I must confess I find no place for olives in chili con carne.

## onions
Chopped green onions applied as a garnish are acceptable and offer a bit of texture and taste that appeal to some. It is not uncommon to find a small bowl of chopped onion or green onion served with chili at good chili parlors.

## others
I've been served chili topped with bacon bits, croutons, and guacamole. If you delight in such toppings, you should add them, but most believe they only detract from the robust flavor of the chili.

## oyster crackers
In some parts of the country where chili is served, the bowl o' red is accompanied by oyster crackers. As with saltines and corn bread, the oyster crackers can be eaten separately or crumbled into the mix. I have heard some claim that nothing goes as well with a bowl of chili as do these little crackers.

## parsley
Chopped fresh parsley is favored by many as a garnish, and a small amount rather complements a good bowl of chili.

## pepper sauce
At the last informal count I took, there were close to two hundred different kinds of hot pepper sauces on the market. The most famous of these, I suspect, is Tabasco. Products like it are often added during the cooking process. Other times, a few drops of Tabasco are splashed atop the chili to add a certain zing appreciated by many.

## sour cream

More and more I am finding restaurant chili served with a large dollop of sour cream on top. Many consider such a thing an abomination, a practice that should be halted immediately. There are those, however, who actually prefer sour cream on their chili and even request it. I can't imagine how this practice got started, for sour cream adds nothing to a good bowl of chili. This odd topping, I am convinced, found its origins in the American South. Indeed, a number of Southern cookbooks that feature chili recipes almost invariably recommend topping a bowl of chili with sour cream.

## tortillas

Tortillas, both corn and flour depending on your preference, are an excellent side to accompany a bowl of chili. Some, including me, have occasionally sliced warm corn tortillas into thin strips and garnished the top of the bowl with them.

## white bread

As far as breads go, there are some folks who prefer plain old white bread with their chili and nothing else. White bread, also called "light" bread, is often a preferred accompaniment to barbeque, but I have encountered a number of souls who also like it with their chili. A couple of white bread enthusiasts told me there is nothing they like better for sopping up the delicious chili liquid from the bottom of the bowl than a slice of white bread.

# the vessel

Discussions sometimes arise relative to the best kind of vessel to use for cooking chili. There are some, the late H. Allen Smith among them, who maintain that a chili cook is less than civilized if he or she does not use a cast-iron pot. I feel much the same way, though I have experienced some good chilis made in other types of cookware.

Somehow, cast-iron skillets and pots seem ideal for such things as cooking chili. I have seen a lot of cast-iron pots at championship chili cook-offs, most often among the winners. A good sign, I maintain.

However emotional you are regarding the subject of a cooking vessel, the ultimate truth is that almost any kind of decent, high-quality cooking pot will work just fine. Don't skimp on price. A cheap, flimsy pot will serve no good purpose at all and can wear out in a relatively short time. A good pot—cast-iron, aluminum, enamel—can last a lifetime.

The combinations and permutations of chili fixins are endless. Over the years, I have enjoyed experimenting with different additions, sides, and drinks, all the while attempting to arrive at the perfect meal of chili con carne. I am convinced I have arrived at several variations that are about as perfect as can be, but I keep experimenting, keep sampling, and continue to enjoy the process that has delivered so much delight and flavor.

# traditional recipes and variations

chapter four

The recipes for chili con carne found on the following pages represent close to 140 favorites, all gleaned from a collection that was started some forty years ago. Many of these recipes came from family members and friends, some were mailed to me during the years I penned a food column, some were developed based on available ingredients, and many were the results of delightful and joyous experimentation. Each one has been tried, tested, modified, added to, deleted from, and otherwise messed with until an optimum pot of chili resulted. The recipes are offered for your enjoyment and your culinary satisfaction.

Following this chapter, which includes traditional chili con carnes and some variations, is a chapter featuring wild game recipes. Wild game—venison, elk, buffalo, turkey, duck, and even rattlesnake and jackrabbit—often work very well in chilis. Since chili con carne is relatively easy to make, using ingredients that are inexpensive, easy to obtain, and easy to store, cooking in camp becomes a relatively simple task. A big pot of wild game chili simmering over a campfire at an autumn hunting camp or a family camping trip can be hard to beat, and some of the fondest chili memories I hold are related to such outdoor experiences.

Recent concerns about fat and cholesterol content have encouraged many to modify their recipes for appropriate reasons in favor of low-carbohydrate and low-fat fare. As a result, I include a chapter of recipes for fitness chili, designed for the health-conscious. Though these recipes can depart radically from the traditional ones, many still utilize fine cuts of meat and chile peppers.

They are delicious, healthy chili-based stews that easily satisfy the palates and health needs of diners.

Here and there in my culinary travels around the country, I have sampled a number of vegetarian, seafood, and "light" chilis, many of which turned out to be quite delicious. I include several of them here and promise you will find them tasty as well as nutritious. The vegetarian, seafood, and other recipes were developed and adjusted with an eye toward eliminating as much of the fat and cholesterol as possible without negatively impacting flavor. Since so much of the taste derived from a good pot of chili comes from the meat, the challenge became a formidable one.

Here is an important hint well known to many chili cooks. For best results, prepare your pot of chili a day before you plan to eat it, place it in the refrigerator overnight so that the flavors will have ample time to blend and meld, and then reheat and serve the following day. It is well worth the wait.

Traditional chili refers to chili con carne made with traditional ingredients employed in the original chilis encountered during the 1880s in central Texas—meat, chile peppers, cumin, and others. The recipes are traditional in the sense that they start with the basic, original ingredients. The beauty of a dish such as chili is that it lends itself well to the individual creativity of the cook. The beauty of a recipe is that it can serve more as a guideline as opposed to an absolute and strict set of rules. Ingredients can be added or deleted as desired, quantities can be altered, substitutions can be made, different chile peppers can be experimented with, and different cuts and varieties of meat can be used. Some cooks prefer powdered cumin instead of ground cumin, some like powdered garlic rather than minced, and so on.

For those who care to depart from authentic chili and prefer beans or other nontraditional ingredients, there are no restrictions. H. Allen Smith, the curmudgeonly chilisto of a few decades ago, stated, "Only a fool sets down precise, unalterable proportions for chili." Chili is to be enjoyed.

# AUNTIE CLARA'S BUNKHOUSE CHILI

Auntie Clara never entered a chili cook-off, but those who have dined on her chili remain convinced that she would have won, hands down, anytime, anywhere. Every Friday evening out on the ranch, Auntie Clara would prepare a big pot of chili, let it refrigerate overnight, and on Saturday afternoon carry it, along with bowls and spoons and a large pan of fresh corn bread, to the bunkhouse so the ranch hands could enjoy a leisurely and delicious lunch. This was back in the 1950s and 1960s, and the hands always said they didn't mind working on fences and windmills ten to twelve hours a day as long as they got to eat some of Auntie Clara's Bunkhouse Chili.

2 tablespoons bacon grease
3 pounds chuck steak, finely cubed
1 8-ounce can tomato sauce
1 14½-ounce can beef broth
7 tablespoons chili powder
2 tablespoons onion powder
1 tablespoon crushed red pepper
2 teaspoons beef bouillon crystals
1 teaspoon chicken bouillon crystals
Salt and black pepper to taste
1½ tablespoons cumin
1 tablespoon garlic powder

In a large cooking pot, heat bacon grease, add meat, and cook until browned. Add tomato sauce, beef broth, 3 tablespoons chili powder, 1 tablespoon onion powder, ½ tablespoon crushed red pepper, beef bouillon crystals, chicken bouillon crystals, salt, and pepper. Stir, bring to a boil, reduce heat, add enough water to cover, and let simmer for 1 hour. Add 1 tablespoon cumin and the remaining chili powder. Stir and let simmer for another 30 minutes. Add remaining red pepper, onion powder, garlic powder, and cumin and simmer for an additional 30 minutes. Serve with corn bread and iced tea.

This simple recipe can be considered a starting point for the culinary inexperienced, at least as it relates to chili con carne. While yielding an acceptable bowl o' red, once mastered, it can be abandoned in favor of more advanced and authentic recipes.

1 pound ground beef
1 medium onion, chopped
1 15-ounce can tomatoes
1 teaspoon salt
1 teaspoon pepper
1 teaspoon chili powder

Using a small amount of cooking oil, brown the ground beef and onions in a cast-iron skillet, and drain if necessary. Add tomatoes, salt, pepper, and chili powder. Stir well and let simmer for at least 30 minutes, adding water if needed.

# BEGINNER'S CHILI #2

Once you've mastered Beginner's Chili #1 and are ready for a bit more adventure but still too timid for a full-fledged pot of regulation chili, give this recipe a try. If you feel daring, add a bit more chili powder than the recipe calls for, perhaps an extra tablespoon or two.

1 tablespoon olive oil
1 onion, chopped
2 garlic cloves, minced
1 pound beef, coarsely ground
2 tablespoons chili powder
2 tablespoons ground red pepper
¼ teaspoon cayenne pepper
1 teaspoon cumin
Salt to taste
1 16-ounce can tomatoes
3 cups water
2 whole cloves
1 green bell pepper, chopped (optional)

Heat oil in a large cast-iron skillet, add onion and garlic, and sauté. Add meat and cook until browned. Add remaining ingredients, bring to a boil, and let simmer for 30 minutes. Adjust seasoning to taste.

# BLACK COFFEE CHILI #1

A number of chiliheads are convinced that adding a dose of strong black coffee to a pot of chili adds dimension to the flavor. This recipe includes not only coffee but a bottle of beer, too!

2 tablespoons canola oil
3 large onions, chopped
4 garlic cloves, minced
4–5 tablespoons chili powder
1 teaspoon cayenne pepper
1 tablespoon cumin
2 teaspoons paprika
2 pounds lean beef, cubed
1 12-ounce bottle of Mexican beer
½ cup black coffee, espresso desirable
½ cup fresh parsley, chopped
½ cup tomato paste
Salt to taste

In a large cast-iron skillet, heat oil, add onions and garlic, and sauté. Add chili powder, cayenne, cumin, and paprika. Stir and cook for another 2 minutes. Add meat, stir, and brown. Add beer, coffee, parsley, tomato paste, and salt. Stir well, reduce heat, and allow to simmer for at least 1 hour or until meat is tender. Add water or beer when liquid is needed. Adjust for seasoning and serve.

# BLACK COFFEE CHILI #2

Here is another chili recipe that incorporates black coffee as an ingredient. Be sure to make the coffee strong because weak coffee affords little or no flavor.

3 dried ancho chile peppers, stemmed, seeded, and peeled
2 dried chipotle peppers, stemmed, seeded, and peeled
3 tablespoons olive oil
2 pounds lean beef, trimmed and cubed
2 medium onions, chopped
3 garlic cloves, minced
1 cup water
2 cans beef broth
1 cup strong black coffee
1 teaspoon oregano
1 teaspoon cumin
1 small can tomato paste
Salt and pepper to taste

Place ancho and chipotle peppers in a shallow bowl, cover with boiling water, and allow to sit for 30 minutes. Heat oil in a large cast-iron skillet and brown beef. Remove and pat dry. In the same skillet, sauté onions and garlic and set aside. Place chile peppers in blender along with water and puree. Place puree, along with broth, in a cooking pot. Add beef, onions, garlic, and more liquid, if necessary, to cover. Bring to a boil, reduce heat, and let simmer for 1 hour. Add coffee, oregano, cumin, tomato paste, salt, and pepper and simmer for another 2 hours, adding liquid if needed, and adjust for taste.

# BLANCO COUNTY CHILI

This simple recipe, according to several natives of Blanco County, Texas, was a favorite of the late Lyndon B. Johnson, a man who surely knew his chili.

2 tablespoons cooking oil
4 pounds beef, coarsely ground
1 large onion, chopped
2 garlic cloves, minced
6–8 teaspoons chili powder
1 teaspoon oregano
1 teaspoon cumin
1 16-ounce can tomatoes
2 cups water
Salt to taste

In a large cooking pot, heat oil and brown beef. Add onion and garlic and sauté. Add the rest of the ingredients, bring to a boil, cover, lower heat, and simmer for at least 1 hour, stirring and tasting occasionally.

# BOBBY JACK'S GARLIC CHILI

This chili recipe was provided by Bobby Jack Childress, one of the finest Panhandle cowhands who ever straddled a horse, rounded up a cow, strung a barbed wire fence, or repaired a broken windmill. His recipe calls for considerably more garlic than most and yields a unique bowl o' red. When I dined on Bobby Jack's chili, I could never stop until I consumed at least three bowls.

1 tablespoon oregano
1 tablespoon paprika
5 tablespoons chili powder
1 tablespoon cumin
1 teaspoon instant beef bouillon
1 bottle dark Mexican beer
1 cup beef broth
3 tablespoons olive oil
2½ pounds beef chuck, trimmed and cubed
1 large onion, chopped
4 garlic cloves, minced
1 teaspoon Tabasco sauce
1 8-ounce can tomato sauce
Salt and pepper to taste

In a large cooking pot, add oregano, paprika, chili powder, cumin, bouillon, beer, and broth. Stir, bring to a boil, reduce heat, and let simmer. In a large cast-iron skillet, heat oil and brown beef. Remove, pat dry, and add to pot. Add more oil to the skillet if necessary, toss in the onion and garlic, and sauté. Add to pot. If more liquid is needed, add more broth or water. Simmer for an additional 2 hours. Add Tabasco sauce, tomato sauce, salt, and pepper. Stir and let simmer for another 30 minutes. If a thicker chili is desired, mix a paste of water and masa harina and add 1 or 2 tablespoons. If a thinner chili is needed, simply add more water.

# BOB'S DRUNKEN CHILI

I have had this recipe for so long I have forgotten who Bob was. Though it has been modified a little over the years, the essential ingredients remain the same and have always yielded a magnificent bowl of chili.

2 tablespoons olive oil
6 fresh ancho chile peppers, stemmed, seeded, and chopped
1 onion, chopped
2 garlic cloves, minced
2 pounds lean beef, trimmed and cubed
1 bottle dark Mexican beer
1 can beef broth
1 teaspoon cumin
1 teaspoon paprika
1 teaspoon oregano
Salt and pepper to taste

After trimming the beef, give the fat to the dog. Heat oil in a cooking pot and sauté chile peppers, onion, and garlic. Add beef and cook until browned, stirring often. Add beer and broth, bring to a boil, reduce heat, and simmer for 30 minutes. Add cumin, paprika, oregano, salt, and pepper. Stir and let simmer for an additional hour. Stir frequently during the simmering process, adjusting for taste.

# BRISKET CHILI

Brisket, not a traditional cut of meat used in chili, is used effectively in this recipe.

2 tablespoons olive oil
3 pounds brisket, trimmed and cubed
1 large onion, chopped
3 garlic cloves, minced
Salt and pepper to taste
1 8-ounce can tomato sauce
1 cup beef broth
1 bottle dark Mexican beer
6 tablespoons chili powder
2 tablespoons cumin
1 teaspoon oregano
1 teaspoon Tabasco sauce
2 fresh jalapeno peppers, minced

In a large cooking pot, heat oil and add brisket. Add onion and garlic and sauté. Add salt and pepper, tomato sauce, broth, beer, chili powder, cumin, oregano, and Tabasco sauce. Stir, bring to a boil, reduce heat, and let simmer for at least 3 hours. Check for liquid and add water if necessary. Fifteen minutes before chili is to be served, add jalapeno peppers. Serve topped with freshly chopped cilantro.

# BUCKSKIN BEAU JACQUES' MOUNTAIN MAN CHILI

The late writer Richard C. House, who contributed this recipe, advised, "Always use a cast-iron skillet or Dutch oven with a domed lid so the moisture can collect and drip back into the mix. Once you put the lid on for the final simmer, leave it alone—too much peeking and stirring allows the flavors to escape. And always stir with a wooden spoon." House was the author of a dozen novels and hundreds of articles, columns, and book reviews.

1½ pounds beef flank steak
1½ pounds pork shoulder (or, if you wish, substitute beef heart)
4 large celery stalks, chopped fine
1 large white onion, chopped fine
1 large tomato, peeled and chopped
1 large can tomato sauce
1 small can green chile salsa
1 teaspoon cumin
½ teaspoon garlic powder
1 teaspoon oregano
2 teaspoons chili powder
1 teaspoon cayenne pepper
1 teaspoon Tabasco sauce
1 can beer
½ cup masa harina

Debone meat if necessary, remove fat, and cut into 1-inch cubes. Render small amount of fat in Dutch oven, add meat, and brown over medium heat. Place all remaining ingredients except beer and masa harina into a saucepan, cover, and cook for 20 minutes over low heat. When done, add to meat, stir, add beer, cover, and simmer for 2½ hours. If increased thickness is desired, mix masa harina with water to form a thin paste and add to mix as needed.

# BURL'S BUNKHOUSE CHILI

This is an easy-to-follow, inexpensive recipe for some fine-tasting chili I got from Cowboy Burl Kennedy. I first sampled this recipe one cold winter afternoon while working on the Escontrias Ranch in West Texas.

2 tablespoons bacon grease
2 pounds beef chuck, coarsely ground
1 large onion, chopped
1 8-ounce can tomato sauce
2 teaspoons garlic powder
5 tablespoons chili powder
1 tablespoon cumin
1 teaspoon oregano
1 teaspoon cayenne pepper
Salt and pepper to taste
1 teaspoon Tabasco sauce
1 bottle dark Mexican beer
2 fresh jalapeno peppers, minced

In a cooking pot heat bacon grease and brown meat. Add onion and sauté. Add tomato sauce and garlic powder, bring to a boil, reduce heat, and simmer for 30 minutes. Add chili powder, cumin, oregano, cayenne, salt, pepper, Tabasco sauce, and beer. Stir and continue to simmer for another hour. Fifteen minutes before serving, stir in the minced jalapeno peppers. Serve with a side of pinto beans and corn bread.

# CALIFORNIA FRONTIER SURVIVAL CHILI '71

This recipe is known around the globe as cook-off champion Ormly Gumfudgin's low-calorie anti-smog chili. For the first time, Gumfudgin's secret ingredient is revealed. During his lifetime, Ormly has been a disc jockey, newscaster, humorist, writer, and chili cook-off contestant and judge, as well as one of the founders of the International Chili Society. Other than chili, Gumfudgin's fame comes from the fact he is the world's only living bazooka player and has been honored for such in Ripley's *Believe It or Not.*

Safflower oil
5 pounds antelope rump roast, marinated in California red wine
4 garlic cloves, minced
2 Bermuda onions, finely chopped
1 cup bell pepper, chopped
1 celery stalk, chopped
5 tablespoons Salsa Brava
20 ounces canned tomato puree
2–3 cans beer
Large handful dried Oriental mushrooms
1½ small cans sliced water chestnuts
2 cans cocktail onions
½ teaspoon salt
1 teaspoon chili powder
1 tablespoon black pepper, freshly ground
2 teaspoons cumin
2 teaspoons ground oregano
2 teaspoons woodruff
2 tablespoons masa harina
½ cup wheat germ

[continued]

½ cup kelp
1 pound white Mexican cheese
2 capsules each vitamins E and A
Secret ingredient

For best results, use fresh spices. Cover bottom of pot with oil and heat. Brown marinated meat for 10–15 minutes, adding oil if necessary. Add garlic, onions, bell pepper, and celery, and brown together. Gently add 75% of Salsa Brava and allow a few minutes for saturation. Add remaining ingredients. After 30 minutes of simmering, add rest of salsa, along with more chili powder if desired. If water is needed to thin the mixture, be sure to use only artesian spring water. Just before serving, add Gumfudgin's secret ingredient—3 pinches of gold flakes—and stir briskly. Gumfudgin claims he picked up this secret in Japan, where it is believed to relieve arthritis.

# CHILI A LA FRONTERA

*Frontera* means border in Spanish, and this version of chili owes a debt to the Mexican influence on cooking near the Texas–Mexico border. Chorizo, one of the principal ingredients, is a Mexican sausage rich in spice and flavor.

3 tomatoes, peeled
1–2 large onions, chopped
¼ teaspoon oregano
1–2 teaspoons paprika
3–4 garlic cloves, minced
4 pounds lean beef, coarsely ground
1–2 tablespoons bacon drippings
20 scallions, chopped
3–4 green bell peppers, chopped
5 hot chile peppers (jalapenos or serranos)
1 pound chorizo, chopped
Salt to taste
6–8 tablespoons chili powder
1 tablespoon cumin
1–2 bottles dark Mexican beer

Mash tomatoes, onions, oregano, paprika, and 1 clove of garlic in a bowl. Place mixture in a large cooking pot along with beef. Heat bacon drippings in a cast-iron skillet. Add scallions, bell peppers, chile peppers, the remaining garlic, and chorizo and cook over low to medium heat until sausage is browned. Add to pot with mashed vegetables and meat. Stir well and add salt, chili powder, cumin, and enough beer to cover. Bring to a boil, lower heat, and simmer for 3–4 hours or until beef is tender. Adjust seasonings to taste.

# CHILI CON CHORIZO

This is another chili recipe calling for chorizo, the spicy Mexican-style sausage commonly found in supermarkets and restaurants throughout the American Southwest. For an interesting change, try this delightfully tasty recipe.

1 pound chorizo, chopped
1 pound pork loin, finely cubed
2 medium onions, chopped
3 garlic cloves, minced
1 red bell pepper, chopped
3 tablespoons chili powder
1 tablespoon oregano
1 tablespoon cumin
1 tablespoon cayenne pepper
1 14½-ounce can crushed tomatoes

In a large cooking pot, cook chorizo over medium heat until done. Add pork loin, onions, garlic, and red pepper and cook for another 10 minutes or until pork is browned. Drain. Add chili powder, oregano, cumin, and cayenne. Stir well and cook for another minute or two. Add tomatoes, mix well, reduce heat, and simmer for 30–45 minutes. Serve with a side of beans or rice and a couple of fresh tortillas.

# CHILI DEGOLYER

E. DeGolyer, as described by H. Allen Smith, was "a world traveler, a gourmet, a litterateur, a sense-making citizen of Dallas, and a gentleman." DeGolyer invested a lot of time studying chili history and lore and worked for years to arrive at the following recipe. DeGolyer owned the *Saturday Review of Literature*, and Smith referred to him as "the Solomon of the chili bowl."

2½ cups fat rendered from beef suet
1 onion, chopped
3 pounds center-cut steak, cut into ½-inch cubes
2 cups water
2–12 pods dried red chiles (adjust amount to taste; may substitute 1 tablespoon chili powder
    for 2 chile pods)
4 garlic cloves, finely chopped
1 teaspoon cumin
1 teaspoon oregano
1 tablespoon salt

Heat fat in a large skillet, add onion, and sauté. Add meat and cook until gray. Add water and let simmer for 1 hour. While meat is simmering, wash chiles and remove stems and seeds. In a separate pot, boil chiles until skins come off (30–45 minutes). Press chiles through a colander to form a paste. Add chiles, garlic, cumin, oregano, and salt to the meat and cook for another hour.

# CHILI H. ALLEN SMITH

H. Allen Smith had the temerity to chastise Texans for their reluctance to add beans and sweet peppers to their chili recipes, calling them "daft." In spite of the many enemies he made, Smith eventually moved from New York to Southwest Texas and became a major contributor to the history and culture of chili con carne.

3 pounds lean chuck, round, or tenderloin, trimmed and coarsely ground
1–2 cans tomato paste
1–2 onions, chopped
½ bell pepper, chopped
1 quart water
2–3 garlic cloves, minced
½ teaspoon oregano
2 pinches sweet basil
¼ teaspoon cumin
2 tablespoons chili powder
Salt to taste
1 can pinto or kidney beans

Sear meat in a cast-iron kettle in cooking oil of choice. Smith says, "If you don't have an iron kettle, you are not civilized; go out and get one." Add tomato paste, onions, bell pepper, and water. Stir and simmer. Add garlic, oregano, basil, cumin, chili powder, and salt. Stir and let simmer for 2 hours, adjusting seasonings to taste. When satisfied, add beans and heat for a few more minutes. Remove from stove and allow to sit overnight. Chili, according to Smith, always tastes better the second day.

chapter four

# CHILI PARLOR CHILI

This recipe was found in a trunk full of papers, menus, and bills saved from an old-time Dallas chili parlor that operated during the 1930s. The recipe calls for what seems like a lot of cumin seeds and chile, but maybe they liked their chili con carne well seasoned in those days.

¼ cup bacon grease
2 pounds lean beef, coarsely ground
1 cup cumin seeds
1 cup dried and ground New Mexico red chiles
¼ teaspoon cayenne pepper
2 garlic cloves, minced
Salt and pepper to taste
1 teaspoon paprika

Heat bacon grease in a large cast-iron skillet, add meat, and cook for approximately 8–10 minutes until browned. Stir in cumin seeds and ground red chiles, reduce heat, and let simmer for 30 minutes. Add water if needed. Add cayenne and garlic and stir. Let simmer for another 2 hours. Add salt, pepper, and paprika, stirring it into the mix. If a thicker chili is desired, mix 2 tablespoons of masa harina with 2 tablespoons of bacon grease and dump it into the pot. Serve with saltines.

# CHILI WOODY

Woody DeSilva was once the manager of the Los Angeles International Airport. This recipe won the second annual International Chili Society's world championship cook-off held in Terlingua, Texas, in 1968.

3 tablespoons cooking oil

5 medium onions, chopped

Salt and pepper to taste

4 pounds beef chuck, cubed

5 garlic cloves, minced

4 tablespoons Mexican oregano

8 tablespoons chili powder

2 tablespoons paprika

2 teaspoons woodruff

1 teaspoon cayenne pepper

1 teaspoon chile pequins, crushed

4 dashes Tabasco sauce

3 8-ounce cans tomato sauce

1 6-ounce can tomato paste

Heat oil in a large skillet and add onions, salt, and pepper. Sauté until onions are browned. Add meat and cook until gray. Add garlic and oregano, stirring occasionally. Mix together the remaining seasonings and chiles, add to meat, and stir well while simmering. Add Tabasco sauce, tomato sauce, and tomato paste. Cover and continue to simmer for 2 hours, adding water when necessary. If a thicker chili is desired, add a bit of paste made from masa harina and water.

# CHORIZO CHILI

This one is similar to precious recipes using chorizo and is a favorite dish commonly encountered in the Texas and New Mexico Southwest. The use of chorizo adds a pleasing dimension. The addition of celery in this recipe, though not a common ingredient, complements the pork and chorizo nicely.

6 dried Anaheim chiles, stemmed, seeded, and chopped
3 tablespoons olive oil
2 pounds pork, trimmed and cubed
2 onions, chopped
3 garlic cloves, minced
1 celery stalk, chopped
1 can beef broth
2 teaspoons cumin
2 teaspoons oregano
Salt to taste
½ pound chorizo

Place dried chiles in a bowl and cover with boiling water, stir, and set aside for at least 30 minutes. Heat half of the olive oil in a skillet, add pork, and brown. Remove meat and set aside; wipe skillet clean. Heat remaining oil and sauté onions, garlic, and celery. Place pork and vegetables in a cooking pot and cover with broth, adding water if necessary. Bring to a boil and add cumin, oregano, and salt. Stir, reduce heat, and simmer for 2 hours. Place reconstituted chiles in blender and puree. Remove skins by straining through a sieve or colander. Place puree in chili and stir. After chili has simmered for approximately 1 hour, break chorizo into skillet and cook until done. Drain grease, pat meat dry, add to chili, and stir. Check the chili from time to time, adding water and seasonings as needed.

# COMPETITION CHILI

This recipe has been adapted from three or four cook-off-winning chilis. Since cook-off competitions generally use chopped meat and forbid the presence of visible vegetables, commercially available powdered and minced onion and garlic are employed for prize-winning chili for friends and family.

2 tablespoons olive oil
3 pounds beef, coarsely ground
1 cup beef broth
2 teaspoons beef bouillon crystals
1 teaspoon chicken bouillon crystals
1 8-ounce can tomato sauce
3 tablespoons minced onion
2 teaspoons garlic powder
8 tablespoons chili powder
2 teaspoons Tabasco sauce
Salt and pepper to taste
1 teaspoon onion powder
1½ tablespoons cumin
1 tablespoon paprika
2 teaspoons crushed red pepper

In a large cooking pot, heat olive oil, add meat, and cook until browned. Add broth, beef bouillon and chicken bouillon crystals, tomato sauce, minced onion, 1 teaspoon garlic powder, 2 tablespoons chili powder, and Tabasco sauce. Stir, bring to a boil, reduce heat, and simmer for 1 hour. Add salt and pepper, onion powder, the remaining garlic powder, 1 tablespoon cumin, paprika, the remaining chili powder, and 1 teaspoon of crushed red pepper. Stir and simmer for another hour. Add remaining cumin and red pepper, stir, and cook for an additional 30 minutes.

# COOPER'S CHILI

Regarded by most during his time as a chili guru, Joe Cooper provided many of us with important information, insight, inspiration, entertainment, and not a few wonderful recipes.

¼ cup olive oil
3 pounds lean beef, cubed
1 quart water
2 bay leaves (optional)
6 tablespoons chili powder
3 teaspoons salt
10 garlic cloves, minced
1 teaspoon cumin
1 teaspoon oregano
1 teaspoon red pepper
½ teaspoon black pepper
1 tablespoon sugar
3 tablespoons paprika
3 tablespoons flour
6 tablespoons cornmeal

Heat oil in a large pot and cook beef until gray. Add water and allow to simmer for 2 hours. Add remaining ingredients except for flour and cornmeal and simmer for another 30 minutes. Add flour and cornmeal to desired thickness, stirring often.

# CROCK-POT CHILI #1

This recipe, like Beginner's Chili, is designed for newcomers to the world of chili, for the faint of heart, and for those with tender stomachs. Once this simple dish is mastered and a desire for better things is evident, move on to some of the more advanced recipes.

2½ pounds beef stew meat, cubed
1 15½-ounce can kidney beans, drained
1 15½-ounce can great northern beans, drained
2 14½-ounce cans seasoned diced tomatoes
1 large onion, chopped
1 teaspoon salt
1 teaspoon pepper
1 16-ounce jar salsa
4 teaspoons chili powder

Combine beef, beans, tomatoes, onion, salt, and pepper in Crock-Pot. Mix well, cover, and cook on low setting for 8–9 hours or until beef is tender. When done, place in a large cast-iron skillet, add salsa and chili powder, and heat for 5–10 minutes, stirring often.

# CROCK-POT CHILI #2

The use of ground beef, beans, sugar, and bell pepper in this recipe suggests that it had its origins in the American South.

1 pound ground round
1 cup chopped onion
½ cup chopped bell pepper
¼ cup red wine
1 tablespoon chili powder
1 teaspoon sugar
1 teaspoon cumin
¼ teaspoon salt
1 garlic clove, minced
1 15-ounce can kidney beans
1 14½-ounce can spiced stewed tomatoes
6 tablespoons cheddar cheese, shredded

Brown meat in skillet. Add onions, bell pepper, wine, chili powder, sugar, cumin, salt, and garlic. Continue to cook until the onion is tender. Place mixture in Crock-Pot, add beans and tomatoes, and stir well. Cover and cook on low heat for 4 hours. After spooning chili into bowls, sprinkle shredded cheese on top.

# DALLAS COUNTY JAILHOUSE CHILI

This tried-and-true recipe had been a favorite with Texans for decades. It is also very easy to prepare.

2 cups beef suet
2 pounds beef, coarsely ground
3 garlic cloves, minced
1½ teaspoons paprika
3 tablespoons chili powder
1 tablespoon cumin
1 tablespoon salt
1 teaspoon white pepper
1½ sweet chile pods, chopped fine
3 cups water

Fry suet in a cast-iron skillet. Add meat, garlic, and remaining seasonings. Cover and simmer for 4 hours, stirring occasionally. Add water as needed and cook for another hour until slightly thickened.

# DOC BLAKELY FUEGO DE TEJAS (FIRE OF TEXAS) CHILI #13

Doc Blakely, humorist, entertainer, musician, and author of seven books, is one of the country's most sought after conference and convention speakers. He also makes a mean pot of chili. Doc says this recipe serves ten normal people or five Texans!

3 tablespoons olive oil
2½ pounds sirloin, cubed
½ pound sausage, ground
4 tablespoons mild chili powder
3 tablespoons hot chili powder
1 teaspoon garlic powder
¾ teaspoon cayenne pepper
1 14-oz. can tomato sauce
1 cup onion, finely chopped
2 tablespoons cumin
¼ teaspoon oregano
10 ounces beef broth
1 bottle dark Mexican beer
Salt and pepper to taste

Heat oil in a large cast-iron pot. Add beef and sausage, brown, and drain. While meat browns, combine chili powders, garlic powder, and cayenne in a small bowl, mixing well. Sprinkle ¾ of mixture on the meat and reserve remainder for later. Add tomato sauce and onion. Stir in cumin, oregano, and beef broth. Cover and simmer for 2 hours, adding water or dark Mexican beer as needed. Add remaining spice mixture, stir, cover, and simmer for another 30 minutes. Salt and pepper to taste. Serve with a side of sliced jalapeno peppers.

# DON'S CHILI

Don Coldsmith is an award-winning author of forty books, 150 magazine articles, and about 1,400 newspaper columns; he is best known for his successful series *The Spanish Bit Saga*. In addition to being a fine novelist, Coldsmith has also been a minister, gunsmith, taxidermist, disc jockey, piccolo player, and grain inspector. He also makes a fine bowl of chili.

1 pound ground beef
1 pound beef, cubed
1 large onion, chopped
1 green bell pepper, chopped
1 4-ounce can green chiles, chopped
3 15-ounce cans tomatoes, chopped
1 15-ounce can red beans
2–3 tablespoons chili powder
½ teaspoon salt
½ teaspoon cinnamon
½ teaspoon cumin
½ teaspoon oregano
½ teaspoon garlic powder
¼ teaspoon cloves
¼ teaspoon pepper

Brown beef in cooking oil of your choice, drain, add onion and bell pepper, and cook lightly. Add other ingredients and simmer for 2–3 hours. For variety, other meats such as venison or pork can be substituted.

# EXPEDITION CHILI

As an avid backpacker who spends days at a time in remote mountainous regions, I have long grown tired of the commercially packaged freeze-dried foods, all of which seem to taste the same, which is to say, like cardboard. There is no rule that says anyone has to dine on bland, tasteless food in the wilderness, so I devised the following recipe for expedition chili. All the ingredients are light and easy to carry. The garlic powder, onion powder, cumin, oregano, and chili powder can be mixed ahead of time and carried in a small plastic bag. This recipe also works well for hunting camp and on family campouts.

8 ounces beef jerky
2 cups water
1 tablespoon garlic powder
1 tablespoon onion powder
1 teaspoon cumin
1 teaspoon oregano
3 tablespoons chili powder
Salt to taste

Cut jerky into ¾-inch pieces and place in cooking pot. Add water and bring to a boil. Add garlic powder, onion powder, cumin, oregano, chili powder, and salt. Reduce heat and simmer for 2 hours, adjusting for seasoning and liquid.

# FAJITA CHILI

The Spanish word *fajita* means skirt and initially referred to a cut of meat known as the skirt steak or flank steak. The Tex-Mex dish called "fajitas" is traditionally made from flank steak, as is this style of chili commonly found in South Texas and along the Texas–Mexico border.

2 tablespoons cooking oil
2 pounds flank steak, cubed
Salt and pepper to taste
4 dried ancho chiles, roasted, peeled, stemmed, and seeded
3 cups beef broth
4 onions, chopped
4 garlic cloves, minced
2 tablespoons oregano
1 tablespoon cumin
6 fresh Anaheim chiles, chopped
1 jalapeno pepper, chopped

In a cast-iron skillet heat oil, drop in meat, and brown. Salt and pepper meat as it cooks. Place dried anchos in blender along with 2 cups beef broth and puree. Place meat in a cooking pot. Add onion and garlic to skillet and sauté. Add to meat, stir, and cook for a few minutes. Add ancho puree, oregano, cumin, fresh Anaheim chiles, and jalapeno. Stir again and continue cooking. Add more beef broth for liquid. Reduce heat and allow to simmer for 2 hours or until flank steak is tender enough to pull apart with a fork. Adjust for seasoning.

# FRANK X. TOLBERT'S BOWL OF RED

Adapted from Tolbert's groundbreaking book *A Bowl of Red*, this chili recipe has become a standard for many chiliheads.

12 dried ancho chile peppers, stemmed and seeded
3 tablespoons cooking oil or beef suet
3 pounds lean beef, trimmed and cubed
1 tablespoon cumin
1 tablespoon oregano
1 tablespoon cayenne pepper
1 tablespoon Tabasco sauce
2 garlic cloves, minced
1 tablespoon salt

Simmer anchos in a pot of water for 30 minutes, remove, place in blender, and puree. Save the liquid and add some to the blender if necessary. Place puree in a large cooking pot. In a cast-iron skillet, heat oil or suet and brown beef. Place beef in cooking pot with puree and add enough of the liquid to cover meat. Bring to a boil, reduce heat, and simmer for 30 minutes. Add cumin, oregano, cayenne, Tabasco sauce, garlic, and salt. Stir and cook for 45 minutes. If you desire a thinner chili, add more of the liquid. If you like a thick chili, add 2 tablespoons masa harina. Simmer for another 45 minutes, adjusting for taste.

# GOAT CHILI

*Cabrito*, or young goat, is commonly raised and eaten in parts of Texas, New Mexico, and Mexico. It was only a matter of time before goat meat was employed in the making of chili. This recipe comes from an American Indian community in northern New Mexico.

2 tablespoons cooking oil
2 pounds goat meat, trimmed and cubed
2 medium onions, chopped
3 garlic cloves, minced
2 jalapeno peppers, chopped
1 bottle dark Mexican beer
1 8-ounce can tomato sauce
6 New Mexico chile peppers, stemmed, seeded, peeled, and chopped
3 tablespoons chili powder
2 teaspoons oregano
1 teaspoon cumin
1 teaspoon paprika
Salt and pepper to taste

For best results, soak goat meat in milk overnight. In a cast-iron skillet, heat oil, brown the goat meat, and transfer it to a cooking pot. Using a bit more oil, sauté onions, garlic, and jalapenos. Add to meat in pot and cover with beer and tomato sauce. If more liquid is needed, add water. Bring to a boil, reduce heat, and simmer for 2 hours. As soon as simmering begins, place New Mexico chiles in blender, puree until a pasty consistency is achieved, and add to pot. Add chili powder, oregano, cumin, paprika, salt, and pepper, stirring well. Serve with fresh corn tortillas, and top with chopped fresh cilantro.

# GOLD RUSH CHILI

The following was adapted from and improved over what is purported to be an original recipe followed by some forty-niners passing through Texas on their way to the California gold fields.

1 large onion, chopped
6 garlic cloves, minced
2 cups chicken broth
2 tablespoons bacon grease
3 pounds lean beef, trimmed and cubed
½ cup tomato sauce
5 tablespoons powdered California chiles
4 tablespoons powdered New Mexico chiles
1 tablespoon powdered ancho chiles
Salt to taste
1 teaspoon cayenne pepper
1 teaspoon Tabasco sauce

In a large cooking pot, simmer the onion and garlic in chicken broth for 10 minutes. In a large cast-iron skillet, heat bacon grease and brown meat. Add meat to vegetables and broth, along with tomato sauce, powdered chiles, salt, and cayenne. Stir, bring to a boil, cover pot, reduce heat, and let simmer for 2 hours. Add water or broth if necessary; adjust for seasoning. Add Tabasco sauce 15 minutes before serving. Top with chopped fresh parsley.

# GREEN CHILE AND PORK CHILI

This is yet another recipe from the New Mexico Southwest and one that is commonly found served in the homes of Indians and Mexicans and in cafés serving New Mexico–style chili.

3 pounds pork shoulder, boned and cubed
⅓ cup flour
3 onions, chopped
3 garlic cloves, minced
2 16-ounce cans green chiles
2 16-ounce cans tomatoes
1 6-ounce can tomato paste
3 cups water
½ teaspoon oregano
Salt to taste

Remove fat from pork and melt in a cast-iron skillet. After coating the meat with flour, add to skillet, brown, and place in a large pot, preferably a Dutch oven. Place onions and garlic in skillet and sauté. Add to meat. Stir remaining ingredients into pot, bring to a boil, reduce heat, and simmer for 45 minutes. Taste and adjust for seasoning, simmer another 30 minutes, and serve with Navajo fry bread.

# GULF COAST CHILI

According to some of my friends who live in the Texas Gulf Coast city of Galveston, this recipe was developed after some seven years of experimenting. They promise the result is sure to please any serious chili aficionado. Be sure to make enough so diners can have seconds.

2 tablespoons olive oil
2 pounds beef chuck, cubed
6 tablespoons chili powder
2 tablespoons minced garlic
1 teaspoon jalapeno powder
1 8-ounce can tomato sauce
1 cup beef broth
1½ tablespoons onion powder
1½ tablespoons garlic powder
1 teaspoon crushed red pepper
Salt to taste
2 fresh jalapeno peppers, minced
1 tablespoon paprika
1 bottle dark Mexican beer

In a large cooking pot, heat oil and add beef. As the meat is browning, add 1 tablespoon chili powder and 1 tablespoon minced garlic. Add jalapeno powder, tomato sauce, beef broth, onion powder, garlic powder, red pepper, and 2 tablespoons chili powder and salt. Stir, bring to a boil, reduce heat, and simmer for 1½ hours. If additional liquid is needed, add more beef broth. Add jalapeno peppers, paprika, the remaining chili powder and minced garlic. Stir and let simmer for another 30 minutes. Check for liquid and add beer, broth, or water if necessary. Adjust for seasoning and serve.

# GUNSMOKE CHILI

This recipe is a favorite of and was contributed by James Arness, star of the popular television series *Gunsmoke*.

4–5 pounds ground beef or venison
4–5 medium onions, chopped
4–5 tablespoons chili powder
1 4-ounce can green chiles, chopped
1 15-ounce can tomatoes, chopped
1–2 tablespoons cumin
1–2 tablespoons ground coriander
1–2 tablespoons red pepper
2 jalapeno peppers, chopped
2 15-ounce cans chili beans
¼ cup Pace picante sauce, hot
3 cups water
2 tablespoons lime juice
½ can beer

Brown meat in a large Dutch oven. Add remaining ingredients and cook, covered, for 4 hours. Add water if needed.

# HABANERO BEEF CHILI

Caution! Habanero peppers are considered to be the hottest on earth. In spite of that, they are also incredibly tasty. If you tend to be sensitive to extremely hot chile peppers, reduce the amount called for. If, on the other hand, you crave the heat of this incendiary pepper, add extra habanero. Keep a glass of iced tea, water, or milk close by. And by the way, be sure to wear some rubber gloves while working with the habaneros, and refrain from touching exposed skin.

2 tablespoons olive oil
2 pounds lean beef, trimmed and cubed
2 medium onions, chopped
3 garlic cloves, minced
1 celery stalk, chopped
2 habanero chile peppers, finely chopped
1 bottle dark Mexican beer
1 teaspoon cumin
Salt to taste

In a large cast-iron skillet, heat oil, add meat, and brown. Add onions, garlic, celery, and habaneros and sauté. Add beer, stir, and cook for another 10 minutes. Add cumin and salt, stir, bring to a boil, reduce heat, and simmer for 1½ hours. If a thinner chili is desired, add more beer or water. If a thicker chili is desired, mix a paste of masa harina and water and add. Top with chopped cilantro.

# HABANERO CHICKEN CHILI

Ever since I have been growing habanero peppers, I have been searching for a variety of ways in which to incorporate these fiery yet oh-so-tasty peppers into a variety of dishes. In the process of experimenting, I have discovered that habaneros and chicken go together very well.

4 dried ancho chile peppers, peeled, stemmed, and seeded
2 tablespoons olive oil
2 medium onions, chopped
3 garlic cloves, minced
2 cups chicken broth
1–2 dried ground habanero chile peppers, according to taste and tolerance
1 teaspoon rosemary
1 teaspoon cumin
3–4 pounds chicken, cut into sections
Salt and pepper to taste

After slicing the ancho peppers in half, place in a shallow bowl, cover with boiling water, and let soak for at least 30 minutes. When anchos have been rehydrated, place in blender with a small amount of water, puree, and set aside. Heat oil in a cooking pot and sauté onions and garlic. Add puree, chicken broth, habaneros, rosemary, cumin, chicken, salt, and pepper. Stir, bring to a boil, reduce heat, and simmer for 1 hour. Turn off heat and allow pot to cool. Remove chicken sections, remove meat from bones, discard bones, and chop meat. Return meat to pot and cook for another 30 minutes. Serve with chopped fresh parsley or cilantro and a squeeze of fresh lime.

# HALLIE STILLWELL'S CHILI

One of the joys of visiting the Big Bend area of Texas was the opportunity to spend some time with long-time resident Hallie Stillwell, who was considered a pioneer of the region. She could be counted on to offer insight on the wildlife, ranching, the weather, and chili con carne.

4 tablespoons olive oil
2 pounds venison, cubed
2 onions, chopped
4 garlic cloves, minced
1 14½-ounce can tomatoes
4 cups water
3 tablespoons Gebhardt chili powder
¼ teaspoon cumin
¼ teaspoon oregano
Salt and pepper to taste

Heat olive oil in a large cast-iron skillet, add meat, and brown. Add onions, garlic, tomatoes, water, chili powder, cumin, oregano, salt, and pepper. Stir well and simmer for 3 hours. For thickening, mix a paste consisting of 2 tablespoons olive oil and 2 tablespoons flour in a small saucepan, brown slightly, add 1 cup water, and stir. Add to chili 15 minutes before serving, stirring often.

# HIGH PLAINS CHILI

The High Plains and Panhandle country of Texas is the source for this recipe.

4 slices bacon
2 onions, chopped
1 garlic clove, minced
1 pound lean round steak, cubed
½ pound chuck steak, cubed
½ pound pork shoulder, cubed
2 cans chopped green chiles
2 tablespoons chili powder
1 teaspoon Mexican oregano
1 teaspoon cumin
Salt to taste
2 6-ounce cans tomato paste
2–3 cups water

Fry bacon to medium crispness in a cast-iron skillet, remove, place on paper towel, and save the grease. Place onions and garlic into skillet and sauté until onions are translucent. Add beef and pork to skillet and cook until browned, stirring occasionally. Add green chiles, chili powder, oregano, cumin, salt, and tomato paste. Bring to a boil, then reduce heat and simmer for 2 hours or until meat is tender and easily cut with a fork. Add water as needed. When ready to serve, crumble bacon, add to pot, and simmer for another 15 minutes, and serve.

# HILL COUNTRY CHILI

This recipe was adapted from one I found at the home of a friend in Kerrville, Texas. While it calls for beef, I have found that it works equally well with pork. Chili powder, red pepper, and jalapeno powder provide for a fiery bowl of delicious red, so keep a glass of something cool and wet nearby.

3 tablespoons olive oil
3 pounds lean chuck, trimmed and cubed
1 8-ounce can tomato sauce
2 cans beef broth
2 teaspoons beef bouillon
2 tablespoons minced onion
6 tablespoons chili powder
2 teaspoons crushed red pepper
1 teaspoon jalapeno powder
Black pepper to taste, not to exceed 1 teaspoon
1 tablespoon minced garlic
½ teaspoon white pepper
2 tablespoons cumin
Salt to taste

Heat oil in a large cooking pot and brown beef. Add tomato sauce and enough broth to cover meat. Bring to a boil, reduce heat, and add beef bouillon, 1 tablespoon minced onion, 3 tablespoons chili powder, 1 teaspoon red pepper, and jalapeno powder. Stir and allow to simmer for 1 hour. Add black pepper, the remaining minced onion, minced garlic, white pepper, 1 tablespoon cumin, the remaining chili powder, and salt. Stir and simmer for 30 minutes. Add remaining cumin and remaining red pepper, stir, and let simmer for another hour. Adjust for taste. If liquid is needed, add beef broth.

# HOTTER THAN A SMOKIN' PISTOL CHILI

This is a peppered-up version of Texas chili that will lift the hat right off your head. The use of jalapeno, pasilla, Anaheim, and arbol chiles provides for a volatile concoction but one that is incredibly tasty.

3 tablespoons olive oil
2 pounds lean beef, trimmed and cubed
1 large onion, chopped
2 garlic cloves, minced
1 bottle dark Mexican beer
1 can beef broth
3 fresh jalapeno peppers, stemmed and finely chopped
1 tablespoon pasilla chile powder
1 tablespoon Anaheim chile powder
1 teaspoon arbol chile powder
2 teaspoons cumin
2 teaspoons oregano
Salt to taste

Heat oil in a cast-iron skillet and brown beef. Remove meat and set aside, then sauté onions and garlic, adding more oil if necessary. Place meat and vegetables in a cooking pot; add beer and broth. Bring to a boil and add jalapenos, pasilla powder, Anaheim powder, arbol powder, cumin, oregano, and salt. Stir, reduce heat, and simmer for 2 hours or until meat is tender. If more liquid is needed, add more beer and broth according to taste. If a thicker chili is desired, add a bit of paste made from masa harina and water. Top with chopped fresh cilantro.

# JALAPENO CHILI

If you like fiery chili but cannot endure the intense heat of habaneros, try this dish made with the equally tasty but somewhat milder jalapeno.

3 tablespoons olive oil
2 pounds lean beef, trimmed and cubed
1 large onion, chopped
2 garlic cloves, minced
6 jalapeno peppers, stemmed and finely chopped
2 cups beef broth
1 8-ounce can tomato sauce
2 tablespoons chili powder
1 teaspoon cumin
1 teaspoon oregano
Salt to taste

Heat 2 tablespoons of olive oil in a cast-iron skillet and brown meat. Remove meat, discard grease, and wipe pan clean. Add remaining tablespoon of olive oil and sauté onion, garlic, and jalapeno peppers. Place meat and sautéed vegetables in a cooking pot. Add broth, tomato sauce, chili powder, cumin, oregano, and salt; stir. If liquid is needed to cover the chili, add water. Bring to a boil, reduce heat, and let simmer for 1½ hours or until meat is tender. Adjust for seasoning and add water if necessary.

# JAY PENNINGTON'S CHILI

Jay Pennington won the eleventh annual International Chili Society's world championship in 1977 with the following recipe.

1 tablespoon cooking oil
3 medium onions, finely chopped
2 green bell peppers, finely chopped
2 celery stalks, finely chopped
3 garlic cloves, minced
8 pounds round steak, coarsely ground
5 cups tomato sauce
5 cups stewed tomatoes
5 cups water
1 6-ounce can tomato paste
1 4-ounce can salsa
1 can hot green peppers, finely chopped
6 tablespoons chili powder
1 4-ounce can chopped green chiles
Pinch of oregano
Salt, pepper, and garlic salt to taste

Heat oil in a 10–12 quart pot and add onions, bell peppers, celery, and garlic. Sauté until onions are translucent. Add meat, stirring occasionally until browned. Add remaining ingredients, mixing well. Bring to a boil, lower heat, and simmer for 2½–3 hours, stirring occasionally. Adjust for taste.

chapter four

# JERRY'S TEXAS RED CHILI

This recipe was contributed by old friend and all-around good guy Choctaw Jim Ware.

3 tablespoons olive oil
2 pounds rump roast, cubed
1 pound pork roast, cubed
3 tablespoons chili powder
Salt to taste
1 tablespoon cumin
1 tablespoon crushed red pepper
1 teaspoon oregano
1 tablespoon Tabasco sauce
2 garlic cloves, minced
1 onion, chopped
3 jalapeno peppers, chopped
1 can dark Mexican beer
Burgundy wine to taste
⅓ cup flour

In a large cooking pot, heat oil and brown meat. Add remaining ingredients except beer, wine, and flour. Stir, and let simmer for 1 hour. If a thicker chili is desired, add flour. If a thinner chili is desired, add beer or wine. Simmer for another two hours.

# LEFTOVER THANKSGIVING TURKEY CHILI

Tired of turkey sandwiches for days after Thanksgiving? Here is an excellent and pleasing way to transform leftover holiday turkey into a delightful chili.

4 dried Anaheim chiles, stemmed, seeded, and chopped
2 tablespoons olive oil
1½–2 pounds leftover turkey, chopped
1 large onion, chopped
2 garlic cloves, minced
1 celery stalk, chopped
2 cups chicken broth
1 8-ounce can tomato sauce
1 teaspoon cumin
1 teaspoon oregano
Salt and pepper to taste

Place dried chiles in a bowl, add boiling water, stir, and allow to sit for 30 minutes. Heat 1 tablespoon olive oil in a skillet and brown turkey. Drain, remove from skillet, and pat dry. Wipe pan clean with a paper towel, heat remaining oil, and sauté onion, garlic, and celery. Place turkey and vegetables in a cooking pot and add broth, tomato sauce, cumin, oregano, salt, and pepper. Stir, bring to a boil, and reduce heat to simmer. Place dried chiles in blender and puree until a paste is formed. Remove skins by straining, and add the puree to the chili. Allow to cook for at least 1 hour, adjusting for liquids and seasonings as needed.

chapter four

# LONGHORN CHILI

This recipe was contributed by Kent Biffle, a former *Newsweek* correspondent and the long-standing and popular Texana columnist for the *Dallas Morning News*. This chili is unique because it uses longhorn beef. Biffle claims this recipes yields "a spicy longhorn chili as tender as a maiden's kiss."

3 tablespoons olive oil
2 pounds longhorn beef, coarsely ground
2 pork sausage patties
2 10-ounce cans Rotel diced tomatoes with chile peppers, lime, and cilantro
1 11½-ounce can tomato juice
2 tablespoons cumin
4–6 tablespoons chili powder
1 cup chopped onion
Garlic powder to taste
Oregano to taste
Salt to taste
1 pot coffee

Heat oil in a large cooking pot and brown beef. Add sausage patties and cook until crumbly. Add tomatoes, tomato juice, cumin, chili powder, onions, garlic powder, oregano, and salt. Stir, reduce heat, and simmer for 2 hours, adding coffee when liquid is needed. Texture of chili can be adjusted just before serving by adding a spoonful or two of paste made from masa harina and water.

# LUNA COUNTY CHILI

I first tasted this recipe while visiting a rancher in Luna County, New Mexico. It reminded me of a cross between chili and posole, a delicious hominy-based stew. It was cold and windy that evening as we dined, but the chili warmed our bodies and souls.

6 dried New Mexico red chile peppers, stemmed, seeded, and peeled
2 dried chipotle chile peppers, stemmed, seeded, and peeled
2 tablespoons olive oil
2 pounds lean beef, trimmed and cubed
2 medium onions, chopped
3 garlic cloves, minced
1 teaspoon cumin
1 teaspoon oregano
Salt and pepper to taste
2 10-ounce cans beef broth
1 16-ounce can hominy

Slice New Mexico and chipotle peppers in half and place in a shallow bowl; cover with boiling water, and allow to set for 30 minutes. In a large cast-iron skillet, heat oil and brown meat, drain, pat dry, and set aside. In the same skillet, sauté onions and garlic, adding more oil if necessary. Drain, remove, and set aside. Place New Mexico reds and chipotles in blender and puree. Place puree in a cooking pot and add cumin, oregano, salt, and pepper. Cover with beef broth, stir, and bring to a boil. Add onions and garlic, beef, and hominy. Reduce heat and let simmer over low heat for 3 hours. Top with chopped fresh cilantro.

# MARTY ROBBINS' CAMPFIRE CHILI

The late Marty Robbins was an award-winning country and western and pop music performer and recording artist, a successful songwriter, and a winning race car driver. This unorthodox recipe includes potatoes and eggs!

3 tablespoons vegetable oil
1 pound ground beef
1 medium onion, chopped
1 large potato, grated
1–3 teaspoons ground red pepper
2 tablespoons oregano
6 eggs, beaten
Salt and pepper to taste

Heat oil, brown meat in a large skillet, and drain. Add onion, potato, and spices, stirring well. To keep the mix from sticking, add a small amount of vegetable oil. When the potatoes are browned, add the beaten eggs to the mixture. Salt and pepper to taste. Stir until eggs are cooked. Serve.

# NEW MEXICO GREEN

This simple-to-make, tasty, somewhat nontraditional dish is made with pork and green chiles instead of beef and red chiles. Commonly found on Indian reservations in New Mexico, it offers a nice variation on the traditional pot of chili.

2 tablespoons cooking oil
2–2½ pounds pork loin, cubed
Salt and pepper to taste
1 large onion, chopped
4–5 garlic cloves, minced
15–20 fresh green Anaheim chiles, roasted, peeled, stemmed, and chopped
2–3 cups chicken broth

In a cooking pot, heat cooking oil and brown pork, salting and peppering as it cooks. Drain, add onion and garlic, and sauté. When onions are translucent, add chiles and chicken broth, bring to a boil, reduce heat, and simmer for 1 hour. Adjust for seasoning. Serve over rice with a side of pinto beans and corn bread or corn tortillas, and garnish with chopped green onions or chopped fresh cilantro.

# NEW MEXICO RED #1

With the proliferation of chile farms throughout parts of New Mexico, the chances for finding some excellent bowls of chili con carne are getting better and better. This recipe for the ever-popular New Mexico red is encountered mostly in the southern part of the Land of Enchantment close to the Texas border.

2 tablespoons bacon grease
1 large onion, chopped
3 pounds sirloin, cubed
3 garlic cloves, minced
4 tablespoons ground New Mexico red chiles
2 tablespoons paprika
2 teaspoons cumin
3 cups water
Salt and pepper to taste

Heat bacon grease in a cast-iron skillet, add onion, and sauté until golden brown. Add meat, garlic, chiles, paprika, and cumin. Stir well until meat is browned. Add water, salt, and pepper. Bring to a boil and simmer for 2–3 hours, stirring occasionally. Taste the concoction from time to time, and add more seasonings if desired. Add water as needed.

# NEW MEXICO RED #2

This simple and easy-to-prepare version of New Mexico red chili was adapted from a recipe commonly used by American Indians residing in the northern part of the state. It calls for Anaheim chile peppers instead of New Mexico reds.

15–20 Anaheim chiles, dried, roasted, peeled, stemmed, and seeded
5 garlic cloves, minced
5 cups beef broth
2 tablespoons lard
2 pounds lean chuck, cubed
Salt and pepper to taste
1 tablespoon cumin
1 tablespoon oregano

In blender, puree dried chiles along with garlic and 2 cups beef broth. In a large cooking pot, heat lard, add beef, and brown, salting and peppering the meat as it cooks. Drain and add chile puree, cumin, and oregano. Stir and cook for another 2–3 minutes. Add more beef broth to desired level, stir, bring to a boil, reduce heat, and simmer for 2 hours. Serve with a side dish of pinto beans and corn tortillas.

# OUT O' SIGHT CHILI

The following recipe came from the genius of Bob Coats, who used it to win the 1999 Terlingua International Chili Championship cook-off.

1 tablespoon Crisco
2½ pounds beef chuck, cubed
1 can Swanson's beef broth
½ can Swanson's chicken broth
1 8-ounce can tomato sauce
2 serrano peppers, whole
2 teaspoons granulated onion
¾ teaspoon cayenne pepper
2 teaspoons Wyler's chicken granules
1 tablespoon Pendery's Fort Worth light chili powder
2 tablespoons Gunpowder Foods Texas Red chili powder
salt to taste
3 teaspoons Pendery's ground cumin
2¼ teaspoons granulated garlic
¼ teaspoon Gunpowder Foods Hot Stuff
2 tablespoons Gebhardt chili powder
1 packet Sazon Goya
¼ teaspoon brown sugar

In a large cast-iron skillet, heat oil and brown meat. Add beef and chicken broth, tomato sauce, and serrano peppers. Stir, bring to a boil, and add granulated onion, ½ teaspoon cayenne, chicken granules, first two chili powders, and salt to taste. Stir, cover, and simmer for 1 hour. Squeeze serrano peppers and discard pulp. Add 2 teaspoons cumin, 2 teaspoons garlic, Hot Stuff, 1 tablespoon Gebhardt chili powder, and Sazon Goya; simmer for 30 minutes. Add remaining chili powder, cumin, garlic, and cayenne, along with brown sugar. Stir, reduce heat, and simmer for 10 minutes. Adjust salt, cayenne, and chili powder to taste.

# PEDERNALES RIVER CHILI

A tried-and-true chili recipe, considered a standard for most chili cooks, and one of the late President Lyndon B. Johnson's favorites.

4 pounds lean beef, coarsely ground
3 tablespoons bacon drippings
1 large onion, chopped
2 garlic cloves, minced
Salt to taste
1 teaspoon oregano
1 teaspoon cumin
2 cups boiling water
1 32-ounce can tomatoes
4 tablespoons ground red chile, hot
2 tablespoons ground red chile, mild

Using a large cast-iron skillet, brown meat in heated bacon drippings. Add onion and garlic, and cook over low heat until onion is translucent. Slowly, and lovingly, add salt, oregano, cumin, water, and tomatoes, stirring as you go. Gradually add the ground chiles until you have reached a taste you are satisfied with. Bring this mixture to a hard boil, reduce heat to simmer, and leave for approximately 1 hour, stirring occasionally.

# PORK AND RED PEPPER CHILI

This dish represents an interesting and tasty alternative to beef chili.

2 tablespoons olive oil
3 pounds pork butt, cubed
1 large onion, chopped
3 garlic cloves, minced
3 cups chicken broth
5 tablespoons chili powder
2 teaspoons oregano
2 teaspoons crushed red pepper
Salt to taste
½ cup red wine

In a large cast-iron skillet, heat oil and brown pork. Remove from skillet, pat dry, and set aside. Add onion and garlic to skillet and sauté. Stir in 1 cup chicken broth and simmer for 10 minutes. Place pork and vegetables in a large cooking pot. Add chili powder, oregano, red pepper, salt, the remaining broth, and red wine. Stir, bring to a boil, reduce heat, and let simmer for 1½ hours or until pork is tender. Top with chopped fresh parsley, and serve with corn tortillas.

# PUEBLO INDIAN CHILI

I have been told that a variation of this recipe is hundreds of years old and was introduced by the Indians to some of the earliest Spanish explorers to New Mexico.

3 tablespoons lard
2 pounds beef, cubed
½ cup flour
1 medium onion, chopped
2 garlic cloves, minced
5 tablespoons ground red chile, hot
2–3 tablespoons ground red chile, mild
½ teaspoon Mexican oregano
4 cups beef broth
Salt, pepper, and cumin to taste
2–3 cups pinto beans (optional)

While lard is melting in a cast-iron skillet, place cubed meat and flour in a paper bag and shake well to coat the meat. Brown meat in skillet, then add onion and garlic. Continue to cook until onion is translucent. Lower heat and add chiles, stirring well. Add remaining seasonings and allow to simmer for 1½–2 hours, stirring occasionally. When meat is tender, serve, adding the pinto beans as a side dish.

# RED RIVER CHILI

From the Texas–Oklahoma border comes this favorite recipe.

2 tablespoons olive oil
2 pounds lean meat, trimmed and cubed
1 can beef broth
2 tablespoons minced onion
2 tablespoons minced garlic
2 teaspoons beef bouillon crystals
2 teaspoons chicken bouillon crystals
1 teaspoon cayenne pepper
½ teaspoon white pepper
2 teaspoons paprika
Salt to taste
1 9-ounce can tomato sauce
5 tablespoons chili powder
2 tablespoons cumin
1 teaspoon crushed red pepper

In a large cooking pot, heat oil and brown meat. Add broth, 1 tablespoon minced onion, 1 tablespoon minced garlic, beef and chicken bouillon crystals, cayenne, white pepper, paprika, salt, and tomato sauce. Stir, reduce heat, and simmer for 1 hour. Add chili powder and cumin, and simmer for another 30 minutes. Add red pepper and remaining minced onion and garlic, stir, and continue to simmer for another 30 minutes. Adjust for seasoning, and add water if more liquid is needed.

# RENO RED

This recipe won the thirteenth annual International Chili Society world championship cook-off for Joe and Shirley Stewart in 1979.

3 pounds round steak, coarsely ground
3 pounds chuck steak, coarsely ground
1 cup cooking oil
Black pepper to taste
¾ cup chili powder, mild
6 tablespoons cumin
6 small garlic cloves, minced
2 medium onions, chopped
2 tablespoons MSG
6 dried New Mexico chile pods, seeded, stemmed, skinned, and boiled
1 tablespoon oregano, brewed like tea in ½ cup of beer
2 tablespoons paprika
2 tablespoons cider vinegar
3 cups beef broth
1 4-ounce can chopped green chiles
1 cup stewed tomatoes
1 teaspoon Tabasco sauce
2 tablespoons masa harina

In a large pot, brown beef in oil, drain, and add pepper, chili powder, cumin, garlic, onions, and MSG. (Although the Stewarts add MSG to their recipes, many cooks choose to leave it out.) Simmer for 30–45 minutes, stirring often and adding water if needed. After pulping the chile pods, add to the mixture. Strain the oregano and beer mixture through a fine sieve, and add the beer to the pot along with paprika, vinegar, 2 cups broth, green chiles, tomatoes, and Tabasco. Simmer for another 45 minutes, stirring occasionally. Mix masa harina into remaining broth, add to chili, and simmer for an additional 30 minutes.

# RIO GRANDE FRONTERA CHILI

The region around the Texas–Mexico border is the area where I encountered this recipe. It's delicious and spicy hot, so you'd better keep a glass of milk or iced tea close by in case you need to put out a fire.

2 tablespoons olive oil
2 pounds chuck, coarsely ground
1 14½-ounce can beef broth
1 14½-ounce can chicken broth
6 tablespoons chili powder
2 tablespoons garlic powder
2 teaspoons onion powder
1 teaspoon cayenne pepper
Salt and pepper to taste
1 tablespoon cumin
1 teaspoon oregano
1 14-ounce can tomato sauce
Pinch of basil

Heat oil in a large cooking pot and brown meat. Add beef and chicken broth, 3 tablespoons chili powder, 1 tablespoon garlic powder, 1 teaspoon onion powder, and ½ teaspoon cayenne. Stir, bring to a boil, cover, and let simmer for 1 hour. Add remaining chili powder, garlic powder, onion powder, cayenne, salt and pepper, cumin, and oregano. Add more broth if liquid is needed, stir, and simmer for 30 minutes. Add tomato sauce and basil, stir, and simmer for an additional 30 minutes. Check for liquids and add broth if needed. Adjust for seasoning, and serve topped with chopped fresh cilantro or parsley.

# SAM'S SOUTHERN CHILI

This recipe is typical of many encountered in the South. It calls for lard, sugar, beans, and hamburger instead of traditional chili ingredients.

2–3 tablespoons lard
1 large onion, chopped
4 pounds hamburger
6 tablespoons ground red chile, hot
2 tablespoons ground red chile, mild
2 tablespoons cumin
3 garlic cloves, minced
Salt and pepper to taste
1 tablespoon sugar
1 12-ounce can tomatoes
1 16-ounce can kidney beans

Melt lard in a large cooking pot, add onion, and sauté. In a separate bowl, combine hamburger, ground chile, cumin, garlic, salt, and pepper; add to pot, mixing well. Cook until hamburger is browned. Add remaining ingredients, stir well, and let simmer uncovered for 2–3 hours. Serve with corn bread and buttermilk.

Breakfast sausage is used to good advantage in this simple recipe.

2 cups chopped onion
¾–1 pound breakfast sausage
2 cups water
1½ teaspoons chili powder
1½ teaspoons oregano
1½ teaspoons cumin
½ teaspoon salt
¼ teaspoon crushed red pepper
2 14½-ounce cans stewed tomatoes
1 15½-ounce can white beans
1 4½-ounce can chopped green chiles
2 garlic cloves, minced

Mix onion and sausage together in a cast-iron pot and cook over medium heat until browned. Add water and remaining ingredients, stir well, bring to a boil, reduce heat, and simmer for 30 minutes to 1 hour.

# SAUSAGE CHILI #2

½ pound pork sausage

2 pounds pork roast, cubed

2 tablespoons olive oil

2 onions, chopped

3 garlic cloves, minced

1 8-ounce can tomato sauce

2 cups beef or chicken broth

4 fresh ancho chile peppers, stemmed, seeded, and chopped

2 jalapeno peppers, stemmed, seeded, and chopped

3 tablespoons chili powder

2 teaspoons cumin

2 teaspoons celery salt

2 teaspoons oregano

Salt and pepper to taste

Break up sausage in a cast-iron skillet and lightly brown. Drain grease, add pork, and continue to cook until pork is browned. Remove meat and set aside. Heat olive oil in skillet, add onions and garlic, and sauté. Place sautéed vegetables in a cooking pot; add meat, tomato sauce, and broth. Bring to a boil, reduce heat, and simmer for 1½ hours. As chili begins to simmer, place chile peppers in blender with a little water and puree until a paste is formed. Remove skins, add to chili immediately, and stir. Add remaining ingredients and simmer for another hour. Adjust for seasoning.

# SOONER GOLD

I am told that this recipe, or versions of it, has won lots of cook-offs in Oklahoma and is popular at Oklahoma University football game tailgate parties.

2 teaspoons cooking oil
3 pounds lean beef, cubed
2 13½-ounce cans beef broth
1 8-ounce can tomato sauce
Tabasco sauce to taste
2 teaspoons beef bouillon powder
1 teaspoon chicken bouillon powder
1½ teaspoons onion powder
1 teaspoon cayenne pepper
5–6 tablespoons chili powder
1–2 tablespoons cumin
1 teaspoon garlic powder
1 teaspoon white pepper

In a cooking pot, heat oil and cook meat until browned. Add broth, tomato sauce, Tabasco, beef and chicken bouillon powder, onion powder, and cayenne. Stir, bring to a boil, and let simmer for 2 hours. Add water as needed. Add chili powder, cumin, garlic powder, and white pepper. Simmer for another 30 minutes and serve.

# SOUND THE ALARM TEXAS RED CHILI

"This is not for the faint of heart," says contributor Fred Bean, the famous award-winning author of forty western, historical, and mystery novels.

2 pounds whole chuck or rump roast, cubed
½ white onion, chopped
⅓ cup ancho red chile powder
16 ounces water
1 tablespoon dried and minced garlic cloves
1 teaspoon paprika
1 teaspoon red pepper
1 teaspoon cumin
1 teaspoon salt
1 8-ounce can tomato sauce
1 tablespoon masa harina

Place meat, onion, and 1 tablespoon chili powder in a Crock-Pot along with 4 ounces of water. Cover and cook on high for 4–5 hours or until meat is very tender. Add the remaining chili powder, garlic, paprika, red pepper, cumin, salt, tomato sauce, and the rest of the water. Cover and stir occasionally for another hour. Mix masa harina in small amount of water and add to pot; stir and let cook for another 30 minutes. Serve with large glasses of ice water or cold Tecate Mexican beer. Desert must be ice cream.

# SOUTHWEST TERRITORY CHILI

James Crutchfield, who provided this recipe, is an award-winning historian and writer who makes his home in Franklin, Tennessee. He is the author of thirty nonfiction books and hundreds of magazine and newspaper articles.

2 large onions, chopped
2 pounds ground beef
2 large cans chopped tomatoes
3 cans kidney or pinto beans
¼ cup barbeque sauce
2 tablespoons chili powder
1 package chili mix
Salt to taste

In a large cast-iron skillet, sauté onions in cooking oil of your choice. Add meat and brown. Add remaining ingredients, lower heat, and simmer for at least 2 hours. Serve topped with cheddar cheese.

# SOUTHWESTERN CHIPOTLE TURKEY CHILI

This recipe puts leftover Thanksgiving turkey to good use. Wild turkey has been substituted on occasion with excellent results.

3 tablespoons olive oil
1 large onion, chopped
3 garlic cloves, minced
1 celery stalk, chopped
1½–2 pounds leftover turkey, chopped
2 cups chicken broth
3 chipotle chile peppers, stemmed, peeled, and chopped
1 8-ounce can tomato sauce
3 tablespoons chili powder
1 teaspoon cumin
Salt and pepper to taste

Heat oil in a cast-iron skillet and sauté onion, garlic, and celery. Place vegetables in a cooking pot, add turkey and broth, and bring to a boil. Add chipotles, tomato sauce, chili powder, cumin, salt, and pepper. Stir, reduce heat, and simmer for 1 hour. Add more broth if liquid is needed. Adjust for taste, and serve with chopped fresh cilantro or parsley.

# STEAK CHILI

Not many chili recipes I've come across call for steak. This one was found in western Oklahoma and leads to a mighty delicious bowl of chili.

10 dried chiles, either Anaheim or ancho, roasted, stemmed, peeled, and seeded
2½ cups beef or chicken broth
2 tablespoons olive oil
2–2½ pounds sirloin steak, cubed
Salt and pepper to taste
4 garlic cloves, minced
1 large onion, chopped
1 large fresh jalapeno or Serrano pepper, depending on taste, minced
1–2 tablespoons paprika
1 tablespoon chili powder
2 teaspoons cumin
1 28-ounce can tomatoes, crushed
2 tablespoons Worcestershire sauce
2 teaspoons oregano
2 teaspoons thyme

Blend chiles with ½ cup broth and allow to sit for a few minutes. In a large cast-iron skillet, heat olive oil and brown the steak. Salt and pepper the meat as it cooks. Remove meat and set aside. Lower heat and sauté garlic, onion, and chile pepper. Add blended chiles, paprika, chili powder, and cumin. Cook for another 2–3 minutes. Add remaining ingredients and allow to simmer for another 1½ hours or until meat is tender. Adjust for seasoning. After ladling the chili into bowls, serve topped with chopped cilantro.

# TASTE OF TEXAS CHILI

As far as I can tell, this recipe, or a version of it, first appeared in a book titled *A Taste of Texas*, edited by Jane Trahey and published in 1949. At the time, it was simply called "A Bowl of Red" and was submitted by a Mrs. C. S. Boyles Jr. Since then, it has seen numerous reincarnations under various names, Taste of Texas Chili being my favorite. Mr. Boyles claimed the correct drink to accompany chili con carne is either strong black coffee or an ice-cold beer.

2 tablespoons shortening
1 large onion, chopped
3 garlic cloves, minced
3 pounds lean beef, trimmed and coarsely ground
4 tablespoons chili powder
1 tablespoon cumin
½ pound fresh unrendered suet
1 tablespoon paprika
Salt and pepper to taste
2 quarts water

Heat shortening in a cast-iron skillet and sauté onion and garlic. Add meat, chili powder, and cumin and continue to cook until meat is browned. Heat chopped suet in a large cooking pot, add contents of skillet, stir, and cook for an additional 15 minutes. Add remaining ingredients, bring to a boil, stir, reduce heat, and simmer for at least 2 hours. Serve with crackers, tamales, or cheese.

# TEQUILA CHILI

Many chili cooks experiment from time to time by adding various kinds of alcoholic beverages to their recipes. Tequila chilis have been growing in popularity of late, and once you try a bowl of this delectable preparation, you will begin to understand why.

2 tablespoons olive oil
3 pounds beef shoulder, cubed
2 garlic cloves, minced
5 tablespoons ground red chile, mild
1 tablespoon cumin
2 teaspoons cayenne pepper
1 tablespoon oregano
Salt to taste
2 tablespoons chili powder
2 cups 100% blue agave tequila
5–6 cups water

Heat oil in a large cast-iron chili pot, add meat, and brown. Stir in garlic, ground red chile, cumin, cayenne, oregano, salt, and chili powder, and let simmer for 5 minutes. Add tequila and water, bring to a boil, reduce heat, and simmer for 2 hours. Adjust seasonings to taste.

# TERLINGUA CREEK YACHT CLUB AND MARINA CHILI

This recipe was contributed by Ginnie Bivona, a writer, editor, and veteran contestant of Texas chili cook-offs.

2 tablespoons olive oil
3 pounds chuck, cubed
1 small yellow onion, finely chopped
2 medium garlic cloves, minced
2 small cans Contadina tomato sauce
2 cans Swanson's beef stock
9 tablespoons Gebhardt chili powder
3 tablespoons cumin
2 fresh jalapeno peppers, seeded and finely chopped
⅛ teaspoon cayenne pepper
Water as needed
Salt to taste

In a well-aged cast-iron skillet, heat oil and brown meat until pink color is gone. Add onion and garlic and cook for a few minutes more, then add tomato sauce and enough beef stock to cover. Bring to a boil, reduce heat, add 3 tablespoons chili powder, stir, and simmer for 1 hour. Add 3 more tablespoons chili powder, cumin, jalapenos, and more beef stock if needed. Simmer another hour. Add remaining chili powder, cayenne, and more cumin if desired. Add water if necessary. Salt to taste and simmer yet another hour or until meat is very tender and gravy is thick.

# TEXAS BEEF AND PORK CHILI

The following is adapted from a championship recipe that includes pork as well as beef.

2 tablespoons olive oil
1 pound chuck, trimmed and cubed
1 pound pork shoulder, trimmed and cubed
2 teaspoons cumin
1 large onion, chopped
2 garlic cloves, minced
1 fresh tomato, chopped
3 celery stalks, chopped
1 8-ounce can green chile salsa
1 8-ounce can green chile peppers
1 teaspoon oregano
1 teaspoon Tabasco sauce
4 tablespoons chili powder
1 cup chicken broth
Salt and pepper to taste

In a cast-iron skillet heat oil, add beef, pork, and 2 teaspoons cumin, and brown meat. Remove, pat dry, and set aside. In a cooking pot, combine onion, garlic, tomato, celery, salsa, green chiles, oregano, Tabasco sauce, chili powder, broth, salt, and pepper. Stir, bring to a boil, reduce heat, and let simmer for 2½ hours. Check for liquid, adding more broth if necessary. Adjust for seasoning. Serve topped with fresh parsley.

# TEXAS CHUCKWAGON CHILI

This authentic recipe is popular in chuckwagon cooking competitions and trail rides.

3 tablespoons cooking oil
4 pounds lean beef, coarsely ground
1 large onion, chopped
2 garlic cloves, minced
1 teaspoon ground oregano
1 teaspoon cumin seeds
3 tablespoons chili powder
1 16-ounce can stewed tomatoes
2 cups hot water
2 green bell peppers, chopped
2–3 jalapenos, chopped
Salt to taste

Heat oil in a large cast-iron skillet. Add meat, onion, and garlic, and cook until meat is browned. Add oregano, cumin, chili powder, tomatoes, hot water, bell peppers, jalapenos, and salt to taste. Stir, bring to a boil, reduce heat, and simmer for 1 hour. As the fat cooks out, skim off the top. Serve with saltine crackers.

# TEXAS RED CHILI

According to Joe Cooper, the first chili recipe ever recorded was credited to Barriga Aleana Corazon Contento. With very few changes, this basic recipe is still popular throughout Texas and the American Southwest today.

2 pounds beef, trimmed and cubed
Salt to taste
8 dried red chile peppers, stemmed and seeded
2 garlic cloves, minced
1 teaspoon oregano
1 teaspoon cumin
¼ cup cooking oil
2 tablespoons flour

Cover meat with water and boil for 30 minutes, adding salt to taste. Save the water. At the same time the meat is cooking, soak dried chile peppers in water for 30 minutes. Remove chiles and save this water, too. Mix the chiles with garlic, oregano, and cumin, and blend or grind to consistency of paste. Add 1 cup of water from the meat and ½ cup of water from the peppers. Heat cooking oil in a large cast-iron skillet and brown flour. Add the chile pepper paste and stir well. Add meat and, if necessary, additional beef water. Bring to a boil, reduce heat, and simmer for another hour. Serve with a side dish of pinto beans along with homemade corn tortillas.

# TRAIL DRIVE CHILI

This recipe is believed to have had its origins prior to the 1880s.

10 dried ancho chiles, roasted, stemmed, peeled, and seeded
4 dried chile pequins, crushed
2 cups water
½–1 cup lard
5–6 garlic cloves, minced
4 large yellow onions, chopped
4 pounds beef chuck, cubed
2 tablespoons cumin
2 tablespoons oregano
Salt and pepper to taste

In a large cast-iron skillet, add anchos and chile pequins to water, bring to a boil, reduce heat, and simmer for 20 minutes. Remove chiles and mince. Save water. In a cooking pot, heat lard, add garlic and onions, and sauté. Add meat and brown. Place chiles in the pot along with cumin, oregano, salt, pepper, and about half of the saved water. Stir well, reduce heat, and simmer for 2 hours, adding more water (or if you prefer, beer) if necessary.

# TURKEY CHILI

This is one of several innovative ways to put leftover Thanksgiving turkey to good use.

2 tablespoons olive oil
2 medium onions, chopped
1 celery stalk, chopped
1 fresh jalapeno pepper, minced
2 garlic cloves, minced
1 pound leftover turkey, chopped
2 16-ounce cans chicken broth
1 4½-ounce can chopped green chiles
1 cup corn
2 teaspoons cumin
2 teaspoons chili powder
Salt and pepper to taste

Heat olive oil in a large cooking pot. Add onions, celery, jalapeno pepper, and garlic and sauté. Add turkey, broth, green chiles, corn, cumin, chili powder, salt, and pepper. Stir, bring to a boil, reduce heat, and simmer for 20 minutes. If beans are preferred, add 1 can of white beans. Serve with chopped fresh cilantro.

# TURKEY CHIPOTLE CHILI

The smoky flavor of chipotle, coupled with turkey, provides an incredibly delicious bowl of chili. Try serving this one to friends on a cold winter's eve. Chicken can be substituted for turkey in this recipe.

4 dried chipotle chile peppers
2 tablespoons olive oil
2 medium onions, chopped
3 garlic cloves, minced
3 pounds cooked, chopped turkey
1 14½-ounce can tomatoes
1–2 cups chicken broth
1 teaspoon cumin
1 teaspoon paprika
Salt and pepper to taste

Cut chipotle peppers in half, place in a shallow bowl, and cover with boiling water. Set aside to rehydrate for 30 minutes. Heat olive oil in a cooking pot, add onions and garlic, and sauté. Place chipotles in blender with a small amount of water and puree. Add turkey to the pot. Add chipotles, tomatoes with liquid, broth, cumin, paprika, salt, and pepper. Stir, bring to a boil, reduce heat, and simmer for 1 hour. Add liquid if necessary, and adjust for seasoning. Serve with chopped fresh cilantro.

# UNCLE ROGER'S QUIEN SABE CHILI

Roger Mears has earned a reputation as one of the finest cooks in Texas and a chili cook-off competitor. He is often called on to exercise his culinary magic in the preparation of conference and convention feasts.

3–4 pounds venison
2 pounds pork, freshly ground
1–2 pounds round steak, cubed
½ cup bacon drippings
2 8-ounce cans tomato sauce
1 tablespoon Tabasco sauce
½ teaspoon cayenne pepper
2 14-ounce cans tomatoes, peeled
1 teaspoon paprika
1 tablespoon cumin
1 teaspoon dry mustard
1 bottle burgundy wine
3 garlic cloves, chopped
3 onions, chopped
6 tablespoons chili powder
1 tablespoon salt

In a cast-iron pot, brown the meats in the bacon drippings for 5 minutes. Add tomato sauce, Tabasco sauce, cayenne, and peeled tomatoes and simmer for 30 minutes, adding water as needed. Add remaining ingredients and simmer an additional 1–2 hours. If a thicker chili is desired, mix a paste of water and flour and add.

# WHISKEY CHILI #1

As with tequila chili, recipes calling for whiskey are also growing in popularity.

¼ cup bacon drippings
2–3 medium onions, chopped
3 garlic cloves, minced
3 pounds lean beef, cubed
2 16-ounce cans pinto beans
1 green bell pepper, chopped
2–3 cups whole tomatoes, peeled and seeded
1 16-ounce can tomato sauce
4 tablespoons chili powder
1 teaspoon basil
Salt, pepper, and paprika to taste
Tabasco sauce to taste
½ cup jalapeno peppers, finely chopped
2 cups whiskey

In a large cooking pot, heat bacon drippings, add onions and garlic, and sauté. Add meat and cook until browned. Add beans, bell pepper, tomatoes, tomato sauce, chili powder, basil, salt, pepper, paprika, Tabasco, and jalapenos. Stir well, reduce heat, cover, and simmer for 1 hour. Add whiskey, stir, and simmer for another 2 hours or until meat is tender.

# WHISKEY CHILI #2

6 dried ancho or Anaheim chiles, stemmed and seeded

1 bottle dark Mexican beer

2 tablespoons olive oil

2 medium onions, chopped

3 garlic cloves, minced

1 fresh jalapeno pepper, stemmed, seeded, and chopped

2 pounds lean beef, trimmed and cubed

1 8-ounce can tomato sauce

½ cup whiskey

2 teaspoons cumin

1 teaspoon paprika

1 teaspoon oregano

Salt and pepper to taste

Cut dried chiles in half, place in a shallow bowl, and cover with beer for 1 hour. Stir from time to time to make certain chiles are exposed thoroughly to liquid. Heat olive oil in a cast-iron skillet. Add onions, garlic, and jalapeno and sauté. Add meat and cook until browned. Place meat and vegetables in a cooking pot; add tomato sauce, whiskey, cumin, paprika, oregano, salt, and pepper. Stir, bring to a boil, reduce heat, and simmer for 2 hours. As chili begins to simmer, place reconstituted chiles in blender, puree to a paste, remove skins, and add to chili. Adjust for seasoning and whiskey.

# WHISKEY CHILI #3

I first sampled this recipe during a cool autumn evening while sitting out on the back porch. Along with the sound of birds calling in the trees and the smells of the season wafting through the air, this chili hit the spot and added to the magic of that day.

2 tablespoons olive oil
2–2½ pounds beef, coarsely ground
1 cup beef broth
1 8-ounce can tomato sauce
1½ tablespoons onion powder
1 tablespoon garlic powder
1 teaspoon beef bouillon crystals
3 teaspoons cumin
2 teaspoons crushed red pepper
Salt to taste
5 tablespoons chili powder
2 teaspoons paprika
1 cup whiskey

In a large cooking pot, heat oil and brown beef. Add broth, tomato sauce, 1 tablespoon onion powder, garlic powder, and bouillon crystals. Add enough water to cover, stir, bring to a boil, reduce heat, and let simmer for 1 hour. Add 2 teaspoons cumin, 1 teaspoon red pepper, salt, the remaining onion powder, and 4 tablespoons chili powder. Stir, allow to simmer for another hour. Add water if necessary. Add remaining red pepper, cumin, paprika, remaining chili powder, and whiskey. Stir and let cook for another 30 minutes.

# WICK FOWLER'S 2-ALARM CHILI

Some claim Wick Fowler is to Texas chili what Willie Nelson is to Texas music. Such important comparisons are always arguable and probably best left to philosophers for debate. Regardless of Fowler's ranking among the world's noted chili cooks, the truth remains that he makes one heck of a fine bowl of chili. This recipe won Fowler first place at the fourth annual World Championship Chili Cook-Off in 1970 at Terlingua, Texas.

2 tablespoons vegetable oil
2 pounds beef, diced
1 8-ounce can tomato sauce
2 cups water
3 tablespoons New Mexico chili powder
1 teaspoon paprika
1 teaspoon oregano
1 teaspoon cumin
1 teaspoon dehydrated garlic
1 teaspoon salt
1 teaspoon cayenne pepper

In a large cast-iron skillet, brown the meat in oil and drain. Add tomato sauce, water, and seasonings. Stir well, cover, and simmer for 1 hour and 15 minutes. Skim off any grease. If a thicker chili is desired, make a paste with some masa harina and water and add to the mix.

# YANKEE CHILI

This recipe was sent to me by a friend who lives in Maine. Though he and the people for whom he prepares chili are partial to kidney beans and hamburger, this recipe also employs a number of traditional ingredients and yields a pretty fair bowl of chili.

2 pounds ground beef
3 tablespoons olive oil
1 large onion, chopped
3 garlic cloves, minced
1 red bell pepper, chopped
Salt and pepper to taste
1 teaspoon cumin
½ teaspoon ground chipotle pepper
1 teaspoon crushed red pepper
3 tablespoons chili powder
2 cups beef broth
1 26-ounce can crushed tomatoes
2 16-ounce cans kidney beans, drained

Place ground beef in a large cooking pot and brown. Drain and set aside. Heat olive oil and sauté onion, garlic, and red bell pepper. Add salt, pepper, cumin, chipotle, crushed red pepper, and chili powder, and stir. Add broth and tomatoes, stir, bring to a boil, reduce heat, and simmer for 2 hours. Add beans and simmer an additional 30 minutes. Serve with fresh chopped parsley and sourdough bread.

# wild game chili

A variety of wild game seems made to order for chili con carne, the flesh from the hunted denizens of fields, lakes, and woods imparting a unique flavor to your creations. Since meat is the heart of chili, many different kinds could be employed in the making of a good pot of chili.

Beef, of course, remains the flesh of choice among a large number of chili cooks, but many outdoorsmen and sportsmen have successfully incorporated venison, elk, buffalo, wild turkey, rabbit, and even rattlesnake and crow into their chili recipes. The results are satisfying and uncommonly delicious, the recipes easy to follow, and the use of wild game in chili simply adds another dimension to the hunt as well as to the kitchen.

# BUFFALO CHILI

Buffalo is becoming a preferred meat among many who like the lower fat and cholesterol content. It is simply delicious.

3 tablespoons olive oil
3 pounds buffalo meat, cubed
1 large Vidalia onion, chopped
3 garlic cloves, minced
2 cups chicken broth
2 8-ounce cans tomato sauce
6 tablespoons chili powder
2 tablespoons cumin
1 tablespoon oregano
Salt and pepper to taste
1 teaspoon Tabasco sauce

Heat oil in a large cast-iron skillet and brown meat. Remove meat to a large cooking pot. Sauté onion and garlic in skillet, place in pot, add broth, stir, and simmer for 1 hour. Add tomato sauce, chili powder, cumin, oregano, salt, and pepper. Stir and continue to simmer for an additional 30 minutes. Fifteen minutes prior to serving, add Tabasco sauce.

# BUFFALO CHILI VERDE

This recipe was contributed by Kathy and Michael Gear, professional archeologists and anthropologists turned novelists. Collectively and individually they have written forty novels. They also raise prize-winning buffalo.

3 pounds buffalo shoulder roast
1 pound buffalo marrow bones
48 ounces canned tomatoes
23 ounces tomato sauce
4 garlic cloves, diced
28 ounces chicken broth
21 ounces Ortega green chile strips, diced
6 jalapenos, diced
½ cup dark beer
Salt and pepper to taste
1 teaspoon cumin seeds
1 teaspoon coriander seeds
1 bunch fresh cilantro, chopped

Boil roast and cut into ½-inch-thick cubes. Combine all other ingredients and allow to simmer for 2 hours. Remove marrow bones and serve.

# ELK CHILI #1

Each year hundreds of chili-loving Texans travel to Colorado and Wyoming to hunt elk and deer. Combining the meat from their harvests with their cultural need for a good bowl of chili, they have developed a number of great recipes. This one has undergone experimentation and modification in my own kitchen until I finally arrived at what I consider the perfect palate-pleasing concoction. This recipe is as easy to prepare in hunting camp as it is in the kitchen.

2 pounds elk meat, finely chopped
2–3 cups water
1 large onion, chopped
2 garlic cloves, minced
1 8-ounce can tomato sauce
4 tablespoons chili powder
1 teaspoon cumin
1 teaspoon oregano
1 teaspoon paprika
3 teaspoons Worcestershire sauce
5 whole cloves
Salt and pepper to taste

In a large cooking pot, add elk and water and cook until meat is tender. Add onion, garlic, tomato sauce, chili powder, cumin, oregano, paprika, Worcestershire sauce, cloves, salt, and pepper. Stir, reduce heat, and simmer for 30 minutes. Check for liquid and seasoning, adding when needed, and simmer for another 2 hours.

# ELK CHILI #2

Try this variation on the previous elk chili recipe.

3 tablespoons olive oil
1 large onion, chopped
4 garlic cloves, minced
1½ pounds elk meat, chopped
1 teaspoon cayenne pepper
1 teaspoon cumin
1 teaspoon crushed red pepper
1 teaspoon oregano
Salt and pepper to taste
1 16-ounce can pinto beans
2 15-ounce cans tomatoes
1–2 fresh jalapeno chile peppers, chopped

Heat olive oil in a large cast-iron skillet and sauté onion and garlic. Add meat and cook until browned. Add cayenne, cumin, crushed red pepper, oregano, salt, and pepper. Stir, reduce heat slightly, and cook for 10 minutes. Add canned beans and tomatoes, including the liquid, stir, bring to a boil, cook for 10 minutes, then reduce heat and simmer for 2 hours. Add chopped jalapeno chiles approximately 30 minutes before serving.

# JAVELINA CHILI #1

The javelina, as most Southwesterners know, is a pig-like animal that frequents the desert areas along the Mexican border. Many years ago, javelina hunters discovered the flesh from this creature yields a delicious taste that provides for a fine pot of chili.

3 pounds javelina shoulder, cubed
2 tablespoons cooking oil
Salt to taste
2 garlic cloves, minced
4–6 tablespoons chili powder
½ teaspoon Mexican oregano
3 cups pork or chicken broth

Using a cast-iron skillet, brown meat in oil over a medium-high heat. Add salt and garlic and mix well. Reduce heat and add chili powder and oregano, stirring well to make certain meat is coated. Add broth to a depth of ¼ inch. Stir and simmer for 1 hour, adding broth as needed. Taste and adjust for seasoning. Cook until meat is very tender, and serve with pinto beans as a side dish.

# JAVELINA CHILI #2

The secret behind this robust wild game chili is the use of smoked paprika.

2 tablespoons olive oil
2 pounds javelina meat, cubed
2 onions, chopped
3 garlic cloves, minced
1 celery stalk, chopped
3 cans chicken broth
1 8-ounce can tomato sauce
2 tablespoons smoked paprika
2 tablespoons chili powder
1 teaspoon oregano
Salt and pepper to taste

Heat olive oil in a large cooking pot, add meat, and brown. Sauté onions, garlic, and celery. Add broth, tomato sauce, paprika, chili powder, oregano, salt, and pepper. Stir, bring to a boil, reduce heat, and let simmer for 2 hours, stirring often. Serve with wild rice.

# LAWRENCE CLAYTON'S VENISON CHILI

The late Lawrence Clayton was the author of several books and articles about cowboys, ranchers, and ranch history. He served as professor of English and dean of the College of Arts and Sciences at Hardin-Simmons University in Abilene.

5 pounds venison, coarsely ground
½ pound beef suet
1 large onion, minced
10 tablespoons chili powder
1 tablespoon salt
1 #2 can tomato sauce
Pepper and garlic to taste

Brown venison in suet in a large cast-iron pot and drain excess grease. Cover with water and bring to a boil. Add onion and seasonings and simmer over low heat for 3 hours. Add tomato sauce 30 minutes before serving. If extra fire is desired for taste, add a few chopped jalapeno peppers.

# RABBIT CHILI

During the times when it was difficult for people of modest means to buy beef, they often had to rely on the bounty of the land to provide what food they consumed. Wild game, including rabbits, often served as an acceptable alternative. Substituting rabbit for beef in chili proved to be well worth the effort.

3 tablespoons olive oil
1 onion, chopped
2 garlic cloves, minced
¼ cup pine nuts
2 cups chicken broth
1 large tomato, peeled and chopped
2 tomatillos, peeled and chopped
2 fresh jalapeno or serrano peppers, chopped
2 pounds rabbit meat
Salt and pepper to taste

In a large cast-iron skillet, heat oil and sauté onion, garlic, and pine nuts. Add chicken broth, tomatoes, tomatillos, and chile peppers. Stir and cook for 30 minutes. As this is cooking, rub some olive oil onto rabbit meat, sprinkle with salt and pepper, and grill over medium heat for 10 minutes, turning often. When it is cooked, cut into ½-inch cubes. Pour chili into bowls, top with rabbit meat, garnish with parsley, and serve.

# RATTLESNAKE CHILI

The first time rattlesnake meat was used to make chili it was probably out of necessity or perhaps as a novelty. Regardless, it caught on, and rattlesnake chili, in addition to being unusual, is good and tasty.

6 dried ancho chiles, stemmed and seeded
2 pounds boned rattlesnake meat
1½ pounds link sausage, diced
1 large onion, chopped
3 garlic cloves, minced
4 4-ounce cans chopped green chiles
4 large tomatoes, chopped
2 teaspoons cumin
2 teaspoons paprika
1 teaspoon Mexican oregano

Place anchos in a pot of boiling water and simmer for 1 hour. Remove from water, peel away skins, and blend until pureed. Brown snake meat in cooking oil of choice in a cast-iron skillet. Add sausage, onion, and garlic. While stirring, add green chiles, tomatoes, spices, and half of the ancho puree. Simmer for 2 hours. When liquid is needed, add beer or water. Simmer another hour, adding liquid as needed. After one hour, add more ancho puree as needed.

# UNCLE CHARLEY'S RATTLESNAKE CHILI

Uncle Charley was a crusty old West Texas ranch foreman who could make chili out of anything. Those fortunate enough to have known him were often invited to dine on chili made from antelope, prairie dog, crow, and raccoon. His specialty, however, was rattlesnake chili. During the summer, Uncle Charley would drive his 1949 Chevrolet pickup truck around the ranch in search of rattlesnakes just to use in chili.

2 tablespoons olive oil
3 pounds lean sirloin, cubed
1 pound pork sausage
3 garlic cloves, minced
3 medium onions, chopped
2 green bell peppers, chopped
1 pound rattlesnake meat
3 15-ounce cans stewed tomatoes
2 small cans tomato sauce
1 bottle Mexican beer
2 tablespoons brown sugar
¼ cup Worcestershire sauce
6 tablespoons chili powder
1 tablespoon oregano
2 teaspoons cumin
Salt and cayenne pepper to taste
1–2 15-ounce cans pinto beans
1 can garbanzo beans

Heat oil in a large cast-iron skillet. Add beef, sausage, garlic, onions, and bell peppers and cook until meat is browned. Drain and place in a cooking pot. After boning rattlesnake meat, add it to the pot along with tomatoes, tomato sauce, beer, brown sugar, and Worcestershire sauce. Bring to a boil, lower heat, and add chili powder, oregano, cumin, salt, and cayenne pepper. Stir well and simmer for 1 hour. Add pinto beans and garbanzos after draining water from cans; cook for another hour, adding beer or water for liquid if needed. Serve over rice.

# VENISON CHILI #1

The old gentleman who gave me this recipe many years ago explained that he sometimes adds all or some of the following ingredients: brown sugar, lemon, mustard, and vinegar. These are ingredients not normally found in chili con carne but, he claimed, actually help in removing the sometimes strong, gamey taste of the venison while enhancing the flavor. For excellent results, try marinating the venison overnight in a mixture of red wine, soy sauce, and vinegar.

1 tablespoon olive oil
2 pounds deer roast, cubed
1–2 onions, chopped
1–2 garlic cloves, minced
2 15-ounce cans tomatoes
3–4 tablespoons chili powder
1 tablespoon oregano
½ tablespoon cumin
1 teaspoon paprika
Salt and pepper to taste

In a large cast-iron skillet, heat oil and brown venison. Add onions and garlic and sauté for 5 minutes. Add the remaining ingredients, stir well, bring to a boil, reduce heat, and simmer for 1–2 hours. If more liquid is desired, add water or beer. Serve with wild rice and steamed carrots.

# VENISON CHILI #2

This venison chili recipe is somewhat unique because it contains mushrooms. 'Shrooms are rarely added to chili con carne and for a lot of good reasons. In this case, however, they have a positive effect, yielding a flavorful dish that fairly explodes with exciting taste.

1 ounce dried mushrooms, shitakes preferred
½ cup bourbon, seven-year-old Jim Beam recommended
2 tablespoons olive oil
2 garlic cloves, minced
2 shallots, minced
1–2 fresh jalapeno chiles, chopped
2 pounds venison, coarsely ground
4 tablespoons chili powder
1 tablespoon cumin
1 teaspoon oregano
1 teaspoon thyme
3–4 cups Mexican beer, preferably Dos Equis
1 14½-ounce can crushed tomatoes
Salt and pepper to taste

Marinate dried mushrooms in bourbon overnight. In a large cast-iron skillet, heat olive oil. Sauté garlic, shallots, and jalapenos. Add venison and cook until meat is well browned. Stir in chili powder, cumin, oregano, and thyme; cook for another 2 minutes. Drain mushrooms and add to skillet, stirring well. Add as much of the bourbon marinade as you wish, along with beer, tomatoes, salt, and pepper. Bring to a boil, reduce heat, and simmer for 1 hour. If a thicker chili is desired, make a paste with 2 tablespoons masa harina and water and add. If a thinner chili is more to your taste, add water or bourbon. Garnish with chopped fresh cilantro, and serve with freshly baked sourdough bread.

# VENISON CHILI #3 (TEXAS DEER CAMP CHILI)

Easy to prepare and incredibly tasty, my first encounter with this version of venison chili was in a Southwest Texas deer camp.

4 tablespoons olive oil
2 onions, chopped
5 garlic cloves, minced
3 ancho chile peppers, stemmed, seeded, and chopped
2 pounds venison, cubed
1 tablespoon coarse-ground red pepper
4 tomatoes, chopped
1 teaspoon cumin
2 cans beef or chicken broth
Salt and pepper to taste

In a large cast-iron skillet, heat olive oil and sauté onions, garlic, and chile peppers. Add venison and cook until meat is browned. Add red pepper, tomatoes, cumin, and broth. Stir and simmer for 2 hours. During the simmering time, stir and add salt and pepper to taste. When I make this for company, I serve it with wild rice, steamed carrots, and cheese quesadillas.

# VENISON CHILI #4 (BREWSTER COUNTY DEER CHILI)

Some mighty fine wild game chili recipes have come from this region in Southwest Texas, and this one has stood the test over the years.

3 pounds venison, trimmed and cubed
4–5 tablespoons flour
3 tablespoons chili powder
3 tablespoons cooking oil
2 large onions, chopped
2 garlic cloves, minced
2 cups tomato sauce
2 fresh tomatoes, seeded, skinned, and pulped
2 dozen dried, ground chile pequins
1 teaspoon oregano
1 teaspoon cumin
1 teaspoon paprika
Salt to taste

In a large bowl combine venison, flour, and chili powder and mix until meat is coated. Heat oil in a large cooking pot and sauté onions and garlic. Add meat and brown. Add tomato sauce, tomatoes, chiles, oregano, cumin, paprika, and salt. Stir well and add enough water to cover. Simmer for 3–4 hours, stirring occasionally and adding water as needed and adjusting for seasonings. Serve with wild rice or roasted potatoes.

# VENISON CHILI #5
## (HUDSPETH COUNTY DEER AND CACTUS CHILI)

The nopalitos called for in this great recipe are pickled prickly pear cactus pads, a long-overlooked culinary resource very few people have taken advantage of.

3 tablespoons olive oil
1 large onion, chopped
3 garlic cloves, minced
2 pounds venison, cubed
1 bottle dark Mexican beer
1 8-ounce can tomato sauce
4 tablespoons chili powder
1 teaspoon cumin
1 teaspoon oregano
1 teaspoon thyme
1 teaspoon cayenne pepper
Salt and pepper to taste
1 11-ounce jar nopalitos
1 15-ounce can pinto beans (optional)

In a large cast-iron skillet, heat oil and sauté onion and garlic. Add venison and continue cooking until meat is browned. Add beer and tomato sauce, stir, bring to a boil, reduce heat, and simmer for 1 hour. As mixture begins to simmer, add chili powder, cumin, oregano, thyme, cayenne, salt, and pepper. Fifteen minutes before serving, drain the nopalitos, and the beans, if using them, and stir into mixture. Serve with chopped parsley.

# WILD DUCK CHILI #1

There are a number of excellent ways to prepare wild duck, but few avid duck hunters I know are aware of its suitability in chili. Contrary to what many chili purists may believe, duck chili is a delicious feast, a remarkable stew, and a recipe that will quickly rise to the top of your list of favorites.

2 tablespoons olive oil
2 onions, chopped
2 garlic cloves, minced
2 duck breasts, skinned, boned, and chopped
2 tablespoons chili powder
2 tablespoons Mexican paprika
1 tablespoon cumin
1 14½-ounce can crushed tomatoes
1 cup chicken broth
½ cup fresh cilantro, chopped
1 tablespoon oregano
Salt and pepper to taste

In a large cast-iron skillet, heat oil and sauté onions and garlic. Add wild duck and cook 10 minutes until browned. Add chili powder, paprika, and cumin. Stir and cook for another 5 minutes. Add tomatoes, chicken broth, cilantro, oregano, salt, and pepper. Bring to a boil, reduce heat, and simmer for 1 hour. Try serving this unique chili over steamed rice for a truly fascinating wild game treat.

# WILD DUCK CHILI #2 (DUCK AND MUSHROOM CHILI)

A chili-cooking friend who loves to experiment with wild game recipes insists that few cultures know how to prepare duck as well as the Chinese, a culture that has long teamed particular spices and herbs with this meat. He claims a wild duck chili should list among the ingredients such traditionally Oriental blendings of ginger, peanut oil, and soy sauce.

1 cup dried mushrooms, preferably shitake
2 tablespoons peanut oil
2 garlic cloves, minced
2 shallots, chopped
2 fresh serrano chile peppers, stemmed, seeded, and minced
1 teaspoon ginger root
2 pounds wild duck breasts, skinned, boned, and chopped
1 tablespoon chili powder
1 tablespoon cumin seeds
1 tablespoon Mexican paprika
2 cups beer
1 can chicken broth
1 14½-ounce can crushed tomatoes
2 tablespoons soy sauce
2 tablespoons fresh cilantro, chopped
Salt and pepper to taste

Soak mushrooms in hot water for no more than 30 minutes. Drain, discard stems, slice caps ¼ inch wide, and set aside. In a large cooking pot or skillet, heat oil and sauté garlic, shallots, serrano chiles, and ginger root. Add wild duck and brown for approximately 7–8 minutes. Add chili powder, cumin seeds, and paprika. Mix well and cook for another 2 minutes. Add beer, chicken broth, tomatoes, soy sauce, cilantro, salt, and pepper. Bring to a boil, reduce heat, and simmer for 30 minutes. Taste and adjust for seasoning. Serve over rice.

# WILD TURKEY CHILI #1

One of the best uses to which you can put wild turkey is chili. The following recipe comes from an Oklahoma chilisto who would rather have his game turkey in a pot o' red than any other way. This unique recipe calls for smoking the turkey before preparing the chili.

4–6 slices bacon
1 tablespoon olive oil
3 large yellow onions, chopped
1 tablespoon fresh cilantro, chopped
1 tablespoon tarragon
1 chipotle or ancho chile, peeled, seeded, and chopped
1–2 bay leaves
2 teaspoons cumin
¼ cup red wine
5–6 cups chicken stock
4 4-ounce cans chopped green chiles
2 cans pinto beans, drained
2 teaspoons Worcestershire sauce
Salt and pepper to taste
2–3 pounds wild turkey, smoked and cubed

In a large cast-iron skillet, cook bacon until not quite crisp, drain, cut into small pieces, and return to pan. Add oil and sauté onions, cilantro, tarragon, chiles, bay leaves, and cumin. After 5–10 minutes, drain, add wine, stir, and cook an additional 5 minutes. Add remaining ingredients and simmer for 1 hour.

# WILD TURKEY CHILI #2

Like the previous recipe, this one comes from the great state of Oklahoma.

1–2 tablespoons olive oil
1–2 pounds wild turkey, coarsely ground
2–3 large yellow onions, chopped
2 garlic cloves, minced
1 28-ounce can crushed tomatoes
1 10-ounce can diced tomatoes with green chiles
2–3 cups water
Salt and pepper to taste
½ teaspoon oregano
1 tablespoon cumin
1 tablespoon Worcestershire sauce
2 tablespoons chili powder
2 cans pinto beans, drained (optional)

In a large cast-iron skillet, heat oil, add turkey, and brown. Add onions and garlic and sauté until onions are translucent. Add crushed tomatoes, diced tomatoes with green chiles, water to cover, salt, pepper, oregano, cumin, Worcestershire sauce, and chili powder. Bring to a boil, reduce heat, and simmer for 1 hour. Add pinto beans if desired, cook for an additional 30 minutes, and serve.

# WILD TURKEY CHILI #3
# (MINNESOTA WILD TURKEY CHILI)

While this recipe comes from a Minnesota friend, it contains some traditional Southwestern ingredients, most notably tomatillos. Added to this delightful pot of chili are great northern beans, which provide an additional dimension.

2 tablespoons cooking oil
4 fresh Anaheim chiles, peeled, stemmed, and chopped
2 garlic cloves, minced
1 onion chopped
2 pounds wild turkey, coarsely ground
4 cups chicken broth
2 cups fresh tomatillos, chopped
1 teaspoon oregano
1 teaspoon cumin
1 teaspoon thyme
Salt and pepper to taste
2 cups cooked great northern beans

In a large cast-iron skillet, heat oil. Sauté Anaheim chiles, garlic, and onion. Add turkey, mix well, and cook until meat is browned. Add chicken broth, tomatillos, oregano, cumin, thyme, salt, pepper, and beans. Stir, bring to a boil, reduce heat, and simmer for 1 hour, adjusting for taste and liquid. If more liquid is needed, add chicken broth or beer. Garnish with fresh chopped cilantro or green onion and serve with fresh bread.

# WILD TURKEY CHILI #4 (CHIHUAHUAN TEQUILA AND TURKEY CHILI)

This recipe returned with me from a successful turkey hunting expedition deep in the Sierra Madres in the Mexican state of Chihuahua. Although the natives who prepared it referred to it as a stew, it had all the earmarks of a wonderful wild turkey chili.

2 tablespoons cooking oil
4 garlic cloves, minced
2–3 onions, chopped
2–3 tablespoons chili powder
1 tablespoon cumin seeds
1 teaspoon crushed red pepper
2 tablespoons chopped fresh cilantro
2 pounds wild turkey, ground
1 28-ounce can crushed tomatoes
½ cup 100% blue agave tequila
¼ cup fresh-squeezed lime juice
1 tablespoon oregano
2 teaspoons basil
Salt to taste
White pepper to taste

In a large cooking pot, heat oil and sauté garlic, onions, chili powder, cumin seeds, red pepper, and cilantro all together. Add ground wild turkey, stir, raise heat slightly, and brown meat for 10 minutes. Add tomatoes, tequila, lime juice, oregano, basil, salt, and white pepper. Stir well, bring to a boil, reduce heat, and simmer for 1½ hours. If more liquid is needed, add tequila. If a thicker chili is desired, mix a paste of masa harina and water and add as much as needed.

# WILD TURKEY CHILI #5

This wild turkey chili recipe has a distinctive French attitude with red wine, mushrooms, and garlic among the ingredients. However, like the previous recipe, this one also comes from Mexico.

2 tablespoons olive oil
3 onions, chopped
3 garlic cloves, minced
1 tablespoon Hungarian paprika
1 teaspoon crushed red pepper
1 teaspoon cumin
1 teaspoon cilantro
1½ pounds wild turkey, ground
2 cups mushrooms, chopped
1 28-ounce can crushed tomatoes
1 cup dry red wine
1 tablespoon oregano
2 teaspoons dried leaf basil
½ teaspoon thyme
Salt and pepper to taste

In a large cooking pot, heat oil and sauté onions, garlic, paprika, red pepper, cumin, and cilantro. Add turkey, stir, and increase heat. Cook long enough to brown meat. Add mushrooms, tomatoes, red wine, oregano, basil, thyme, salt, and pepper. Bring to a boil, reduce heat, and let simmer for 1½ hours. Stir occasionally and adjust for taste. If thicker chili is desired, add a paste made from masa harina and water. If a thinner chili is desired, add chicken broth.

# WILD TURKEY CHILI #6 (MOUNTAIN MAN TURKEY CHILI)

This recipe was adapted from one given to me by an avid wild turkey hunter who prepared this dish in camp, always to the rousing cheers of his companions. The recipe was also tested using leftover Thanksgiving turkey with excellent results.

4 dried Anaheim chile peppers, stemmed, seeded, peeled, and chopped
4 tablespoons olive oil
2 pounds turkey meat, finely chopped
2 cups chicken broth
1 large onion, chopped
2 garlic cloves, minced
1 celery stalk, chopped
2 fresh jalapeno peppers, chopped
1 15-ounce can crushed tomatoes
½ teaspoon sage
1 teaspoon oregano
Salt and pepper to taste
1 15-ounce can kidney beans

Place dried Anaheim chiles in a bowl and cover with boiling water, stir, and set aside for 30 minutes. Heat 2 tablespoons olive oil in a cast-iron skillet, add turkey, and brown. Drain, pat meat dry with paper towels, and place into cooking pot. Add chicken broth, bring to a boil, reduce heat, and simmer. Wipe residue from skillet with a paper towel, and heat remaining olive oil. Add onion, garlic, and celery and sauté. Add to the pot along with jalapeno peppers, tomatoes including liquid, sage, oregano, salt, and pepper. Stir, bring to a boil, reduce heat, and simmer for 1 hour. As the simmering process begins, mash the reconstituted chile peppers, add to the pot, and stir. Fifteen minutes before serving, add kidney beans. Adjust for seasoning.

# notes

_____

_____

_____

_____

_____

_____

_____

_____

_____

_____

_____

_____

_____

_____

_____

# fitness chili

chapter six

To many who claim to be dyed-in-the-wool chili con carne cooks and diners, the notion of preparing this special and culturally significant dish using seafood or only vegetables may, at first, seem absurd. Because of the growing awareness of the consequences of too much fat and cholesterol, however, cooks and chefs have begun developing new and exciting recipes in order to address these increasing concerns.

Although the nation's fraternity of professional and committed chili cooks tends to be a rather conservative lot, a growing number who possess a distinct sense of adventure and a zest for trying something new are finding a lot of good things to say about seafood chili and vegetarian chili.

The following recipes show some delicious and exciting chili variations with bass, scallops, shrimp, and crabmeat. But the challenge, according to many, comes from trying to prepare a pot of chili with no beef or pork. In order to create a high-quality pot of chili, one that can hold its own with those who are fanatic about taste, bold approaches to altering and adding certain ingredients are called for. A lot of work and experimentation went into testing quantities and kinds of chile peppers as well as other ingredients. Experiments and adventures of this nature are continuing, but I am delighted so far with the results presented on the following pages.

# BASS GRILL CHILI

This is another recipe adapted from a Mexican dish. In this case, it was discovered in a quiet little restaurant near the shores of Lake Boquillas in the state of Chihuahua. Cooks perform some innovative magic with bass and chile peppers down there, and this is one of them.

3 tablespoons cooking oil
2 tablespoons chili powder
1 teaspoon Mexican paprika
2 pounds black bass filets
1 cup fish broth
1–2 cups cooked pinto beans
1 cup green chiles, chopped
Salt and white pepper to taste

In a bowl, mix oil, chili powder, and paprika. Dredge bass filets through this mixture, assuring each piece is well coated. Grill 7–8 minutes on each side over medium heat. In a cooking pot, combine broth, pinto beans, green chiles, salt, and white pepper. Stir well and cook for several minutes. Spoon the mix into a shallow bowl, place the grilled bass on top, and serve with fresh chopped cilantro.

# BEAN CHILI A LA BIRMINGHAM

While the pinto bean is the legume of choice in Texas and the American Southwest, the black-eyed pea dominates in much of the South. The following recipe, as far as I can ascertain, had its origins in Birmingham, Alabama, but was experimented with and refined in various West Texas kitchens. The original Birmingham version called for sugar and vinegar, neither of which contributed much to the dish, so I eliminated them. If your tastes run in that direction, however, feel free to add them.

4 pounds fresh black-eyed peas
3 tablespoons olive oil
2 onions, chopped
2 garlic cloves, minced
4 fresh Anaheim chiles, stemmed, seeded, and chopped
2 fresh jalapeno chiles, stemmed, seeded, and chopped
1 pound fresh tomatoes, peeled and chopped
¼ cup fresh cilantro, chopped
2 tablespoons oregano
Salt and pepper to taste

In a cooking pot, add black-eyed peas to boiling water and cook for 2–3 minutes. Drain, rinse, and set aside while you prepare the other ingredients. In a cast-iron skillet, heat olive oil and sauté onions, garlic, and chile peppers. Add black-eyed peas, tomatoes, cilantro, oregano, salt, and pepper; cook for another 10–15 minutes or until peas are tender. This yields a relatively thick chili. If a thinner one is desired, add some tomato juice. In Birmingham, they serve this over rice and garnish it with chopped fresh parsley or cilantro.

# BEAN CHILI A LA CHICAGO

In those parts of the country with significant populations of vegetarians, you can also find some innovative recipes for a variety of meatless chili dishes. The following recipe was encountered in a health food restaurant in suburban Chicago.

1 pound dried great northern beans
2 tablespoons olive oil
2 onions, chopped
3 garlic cloves, minced
4 fresh Anaheim chile peppers, stemmed, peeled, and chopped
2 fresh jalapeno peppers, stemmed, peeled, and chopped
1 tablespoon cumin
1 teaspoon crushed red pepper
6 cups chicken broth
2 cups sun-dried tomatoes
2 tablespoons oregano
1 cup parsley
Salt and pepper to taste

In a cooking pot, cover great northern beans with water and bring to a boil; cook for 5 minutes. Remove pot and set aside, allowing beans to soak for 1 hour. While beans are soaking, heat olive oil and sauté onions, garlic, and chile peppers. Add cumin and red pepper, stir, and cook for 1 minute. Add beans, including the water, and chicken broth; stir well and bring to a boil. While you are waiting for the mix to boil, stir in 1 cup sun-dried tomatoes, oregano, parsley, salt, and pepper. Reduce heat and let simmer for 2 hours or until beans are tender. At that point, add the last cup of sun-dried tomatoes, cook for 15 minutes, and serve with homemade wheat crackers.

# BEAN CHILI A LA THIBODEAUX

This vegetarian chili dish was discovered one early morning in a Thibodeaux, Louisiana, eatery. I traded a Pedernales River Chili recipe for it. This recipe represents a tasty variation on traditional chili, and it's one I enjoy on cold winter evenings. Different peppers can be substituted for the cayennes.

1 pound dried red or pinto beans
2 tablespoons olive oil
2 onions, chopped
2 garlic cloves, minced
1 celery stalk, chopped
3–4 fresh cayenne peppers, stemmed, seeded, and chopped
2 tablespoons cumin
1 14½-ounce can crushed tomatoes
4 tomato cans of water
½ cup fresh cilantro, chopped
1 teaspoon oregano
Salt and pepper to taste

Place beans in a cooking pot, cover with water, bring to a boil, cook for 5–10 minutes, and set aside. After 1 hour, dump beans into a colander, drain, rinse, and allow them to dry a bit in the sink while you prepare the other ingredients. In a large cast-iron skillet, heat oil and sauté onions, garlic, celery, and chile peppers. Add cumin, stir, and cook for 2 minutes. Add beans, tomatoes, water, cilantro, oregano, salt, and pepper. Stir, bring to a boil, reduce heat, and simmer for 2½ hours or until beans are tender. Serve over rice, and garnish with parsley and Tabasco sauce.

# BLACK BEAN CHILI A LA TEXAS GULF COAST

This simple recipe takes only minutes to prepare.

2 tablespoons olive oil
1 large onion, chopped
2 garlic cloves, minced
2 15-ounce cans black beans
2–3 cups chicken broth
Salt and pepper to taste
1 teaspoon cumin

Heat oil in a cooking pot, add onion and garlic, and sauté. Add beans, chicken broth, salt, and pepper; bring to a boil, reduce heat, and simmer for 30 minutes. Add cumin, stir, and cook for an additional 10 minutes. Serve over rice, and top with chopped green onions.

# BLACK BEAN VEGETARIAN CHILI

The following is yet another variation of bean-based, meatless chili.

2 cups black beans
2 Anaheim chile peppers, stemmed, seeded, peeled, and chopped
2 tablespoons olive oil
2 medium onions, chopped
2 garlic cloves, minced
1 celery stalk, chopped
2 tablespoons chili powder
2 teaspoons cumin
2 teaspoons oregano
1 28-ounce can tomatoes, crushed
Salt and pepper to taste

After soaking beans overnight in salted water, drain, rinse, place in a large cooking pot, cover with fresh cold water, and bring to a boil. Reduce heat and let simmer. Cut Anaheim chile peppers in half, place in a shallow bowl, cover with boiling water, stir, and allow to set for 45 minutes. Heat olive oil in a skillet and sauté onions, garlic, and celery. Stir in chili powder, cumin, and oregano, and cook for another 2 minutes. When finished, place in pot with beans. Transfer the Anaheims to a blender, add ½ cup tomatoes, and puree. Add puree to pot, along with the remaining tomatoes. Continue to simmer for 2 hours or until beans are tender, adding salt and pepper as you go. Serve topped with fresh parsley, green onions, and cilantro.

# CAJUN SHRIMP CHILI

In the opinion of many, some of the finest cooks in the country are found in southern Louisiana. The following recipe is a result of my numerous trips to Cajun country and exploring the various ways of preparing shrimp.

4 tablespoons olive oil
1 onion, chopped
2 garlic cloves, minced
6 fresh chiles, Anaheim or ancho or jalapeno, stemmed, seeded, and chopped
2 cups cooked great northern beans
4 cups fish broth
2 cups tomatillos, chopped
1 tablespoon oregano
1 teaspoon dried leaf basil
1 teaspoon thyme
Salt and white pepper to taste
2 tablespoons chili powder
1 tablespoon Mexican paprika
1½–2 pounds fresh shrimp, peeled

In a cooking pot, heat olive oil and sauté onion, garlic, and chile peppers. Add beans, broth, tomatillos, oregano, basil, thyme, salt, and pepper. Stir, bring to a boil, reduce heat, and simmer for 30 minutes. If needed, add liquid (water or beer). Add chili powder and paprika, stir, and simmer for 15 minutes. Rub shrimp with butter, season with paprika, and sauté in lightly buttered pan until blackened. Add to chili mixture, stir, and serve with chopped cilantro garnish.

# CARLOS' LOBSTER CHILI

As a result of a dare, I arrived at the following recipe that includes lobster and black beans. It proved to be immensely popular with guests who continue to request it.

3 tablespoons olive oil
4 shallots, chopped
2 garlic cloves, minced
10 fresh ancho chile peppers, stemmed, seeded, peeled, and chopped
1 cup cooked black beans
2 cups fish broth
1 14½-ounce can crushed tomatoes
1 tablespoon oregano
½ tablespoon basil
1 teaspoon thyme
Salt and pepper to taste
4 lobster tails
½ stick butter, melted
2 tablespoons Hungarian paprika

In a cast-iron skillet, heat oil and sauté shallots, garlic, and chile peppers. Place in a cooking pot and add beans, fish broth, tomatoes, oregano, basil, thyme, salt, and pepper. Bring to a boil, reduce heat, and simmer for 30 minutes. In a separate saucepan, boil water and blanche lobster tails, drain, shell, and pat dry. Cut tails into ¾-inch slices, place in a shallow dish, and add melted butter, making certain pieces are well coated. Season with paprika and grill for 1 minute each side. Serve the chili mix in bowls, top with lobster, and garnish with fresh-chopped cilantro or parsley.

# CATFISH CHILI

10 dried ancho or Anaheim chiles, stemmed, seeded, and roasted
2 cups fish broth
3 tablespoons olive oil
4 medium shallots, chopped
2 garlic cloves, minced
1 teaspoon cumin
4 tomatoes, chopped
2 teaspoons oregano
1 teaspoon basil
Salt and pepper to taste
2 tablespoons chili powder
1 teaspoon coriander
2 pounds catfish filets

Place dried chiles in a blender along with 1 cup of fish broth and process until pureed. In a large skillet, heat oil, add shallots and garlic, and sauté. Stir in cumin, cook for another 10 minutes, and add pureed chiles. Mix well and cook for 2 more minutes. Add remaining fish broth, tomatoes, oregano, basil, salt, and pepper. Bring to a boil, reduce heat, and simmer for 30 minutes or until sauce has thickened. In a bowl, mix chili powder and coriander. Rub this mixture onto the catfish, and grill for approximately 5 minutes per side. When fish is done, cut into pieces and add to mix. Cook for another 10 minutes, then serve over rice and garnish with rosemary, chives, or chopped fresh cilantro.

# CHICKEN BREAST AND WHITE BEAN CHILI

This recipe is filled with nutritious low-calorie and low-cholesterol ingredients.

2 cups white beans
2 tablespoons chili powder
1 teaspoon cumin
1 teaspoon oregano
1 teaspoon cayenne pepper
1 teaspoon thyme
3–4 chicken breasts, skinned, boned, and cubed
2 tablespoons olive oil
1 onion, chopped
2 garlic cloves, minced
1 celery stalk, chopped
2 cups chicken broth
4 ancho chile peppers, stemmed, seeded, peeled, and chopped
Salt and pepper to taste

Soak beans overnight, drain, place in a pot, and cover with fresh cold water. Bring to a boil, reduce heat, and simmer. In a bowl, mix chili powder, cumin, oregano, cayenne, and thyme. Add chicken and toss, making certain each cube of meat is coated with spices. In a large skillet, heat oil and sauté onion, garlic, and celery. Place sautéed vegetables into the pot of beans. Add more oil to skillet if necessary, add chicken, and cook until meat is browned, stirring occasionally. Place chicken into pot of beans, add chicken broth and chopped anchos, stir, and simmer for 2 hours or until beans are tender. Add salt and pepper to taste. If liquid is needed, add more chicken broth. Adjust for seasoning and serve with chopped parsley.

# CRABMEAT CHILI

Fresh crabmeat is best if you can get it, but a few recent experiments with canned crabmeat have proved satisfactory.

6 tablespoons unsalted butter
4 tablespoons olive oil
1 shallot, chopped
1 garlic clove, minced
2 teaspoons dried red chiles, crushed
1 teaspoon paprika
1 pound crabmeat, shredded
Salt and white pepper to taste

In a cooking pot, heat unsalted butter and olive oil, add shallot and garlic, and sauté. Add crushed red chiles and paprika, stir, and cook for another 2 minutes. Add crabmeat, salt, and pepper. Mix well, and cook for another 10 minutes. Serve over rice, and garnish with chopped fresh cilantro.

# EGGPLANT CHILI

This recipe substitutes eggplant for meat and is delicious.

3 medium eggplant, cut into ¾-inch slices
4–6 tablespoons olive oil
Salt, pepper, and paprika to taste
2 onions, chopped
2 garlic cloves, minced
4 fresh ancho or Anaheim chile peppers, stemmed, seeded, and chopped
4 tablespoons chili powder
3–4 tomatoes, chopped
2 green bell peppers, chopped
¼ cup tomato paste
1 tablespoon oregano
1 tablespoon thyme

After coating eggplant slices with olive oil, sprinkle with salt, pepper, and paprika. Grill over medium heat for no more than 10 minutes, turning often. Remove from grill and set aside. In a cooking pot, heat remaining oil and sauté onions, garlic, and chile peppers. Reduce heat, add chili powder, stir, and cook for an additional 2 minutes. Add tomatoes, bell pepper, tomato paste, oregano, thyme, and additional salt, pepper, and paprika if desired. Stir and let cook for 10 minutes. Cut eggplant slices into 1-inch pieces, add to mix, and cook for another 5 minutes. Rice is an excellent accompaniment to this dish, either on the side or with the chili poured on top. A dry white wine is an excellent complement to this dish.

# GARBANZO AND PINTO BEAN CHILI

For a meatless chili, this one packs a lot of flavor and possesses an exciting texture. Feel free to substitute kidney beans for pinto beans if you desire.

1½ cups dried garbanzo beans
1½ cups dried pinto beans
2 tablespoons olive oil
1 large onion, chopped
3 garlic cloves, minced
1 celery stalk, chopped
1 15-ounce can crushed tomatoes
1 8-ounce can tomato sauce
4 ancho chiles, stemmed, seeded, peeled, and chopped
2 tablespoons chili powder
2 teaspoons cumin
2 teaspoons oregano
Salt to taste
2 serrano chile peppers, finely chopped

Soak garbanzo beans and pinto beans overnight in salted water. Drain, place in a cooking pot, and
cover with fresh cold water. Bring to a boil, reduce heat, and simmer. Heat oil in a cast-iron skillet
and sauté onions, garlic, and celery. Add to beans along with tomatoes, tomato sauce, anchos, chili
powder, cumin, oregano, and salt to taste. Stir and simmer for another 1½ hours or until beans are
tender. Add liquid if necessary, and adjust for seasoning. Fifteen minutes before serving, add serrano
peppers and stir. Serve topped with fresh chopped cilantro or green onion.

# GARDEN CHILI

The following recipe is the product of a committee. Several of us with backyard gardens pooled our harvest one weekend and responded to the challenge of preparing a vegetarian chili. The result was a hit.

2 tablespoons olive oil
1 large onion, chopped
1 green bell pepper, chopped
1 cup mushrooms, chopped
4 fresh jalapeno peppers, stemmed and chopped
3 tablespoons chili powder
1 tablespoon oregano
1 teaspoon cumin
2 cups water
½ cup uncooked cracked wheat
2 14½-ounce cans diced tomatoes
1 10-ounce can tomato puree
1 cup corn
2 16-ounce cans white beans

Heat oil in a large cooking pot. Sauté onion, bell pepper, mushrooms, jalapenos, chili powder, oregano, and cumin. Add water, cracked wheat, tomatoes, and tomato puree. Stir, bring to a boil, reduce heat, and simmer for 30 minutes. Add corn and beans, cook another 10 minutes, and serve. Garnish with chopped parsley or cilantro.

# HEALTHY CHICKEN CHILI

This is another one of my favorite low-calorie recipes

2 tablespoons olive oil
1 pound chicken, cubed
1 large onion, chopped
1 green bell pepper, chopped
1–2 fresh jalapeno peppers, stemmed and chopped
½ cup sun-dried tomatoes
2 tablespoons chili powder
1 tablespoon cumin
2 teaspoons oregano
3 garlic cloves, minced
2 cups water
1 cup dried pinto beans
2 large fresh tomatoes, peeled and chopped
1 cup corn (fresh is preferred, but canned will do)
Salt and ground red pepper to taste

In a large cooking pot, heat oil, add chicken and onion, and cook for 2–3 minutes. Add bell pepper, jalapenos, dried tomatoes, chili powder, cumin, oregano, and garlic. Cook over medium heat for 2 minutes. Add water and dried beans. Bring to a boil, cover, reduce heat, and simmer for 1–2 hours or until beans are tender. Add fresh tomatoes, corn, salt, and red pepper. Stir well, return to a boil, cook for another 5–10 minutes, and serve.

# LOW-FAT TEXAS CHILI WITH BEEF

The use of a small amount of lean beef in this low-calorie recipe provides a great burst of taste.

1 tablespoon olive oil
½ pound very lean sirloin, cubed
1 large onion, chopped
1 green bell pepper, chopped
1 8-ounce can tomato sauce
1 13½-ounce can beef broth
1 6-ounce can tomato paste
1–2 tablespoons chili powder
1 teaspoon cumin
2 16-ounce cans pinto beans

In a large cast-iron skillet, heat oil and brown beef. Add onion and green pepper, and cook over medium heat until beef is done. Drain. Add tomato sauce, beef broth, tomato paste, chili powder, cumin, and beans. Stir well and simmer for at least 1 hour. Adjust seasonings to taste.

# MUSHROOM CHILI

More and more I am encountering vegetarian friends who substitute mushrooms for meat on a regular basis. Some portobello burgers I've consumed lately were entirely satisfying, and several different varieties of meatless pasta sauce made with mushrooms have likewise been delectable.

4 tablespoons olive oil
4 onions, chopped
4 garlic cloves, minced
4 tablespoons chili powder
1 tablespoon cumin
3 pounds fresh mushrooms, chopped
2 green or red bell peppers, chopped
½ cup tomato paste
2 tablespoons dried leaf oregano
1 tablespoon dried leaf basil
Salt and pepper to taste

In a cooking pot, heat olive oil, add onions and garlic, and sauté. Add chili powder and cumin, stir, and cook for another minute. Add mushrooms and cook over medium heat for 15 minutes. Add bell peppers, tomato paste, oregano, basil, salt, and pepper. Mix well and cook for 10 minutes. If more liquid is needed, add tomato juice or beer. If a thicker chili is desired, add a paste made from masa harina and water.

# PEAK OF HEALTH VEGETARIAN CHILI

Vegetarian chili offers the challenge of maintaining a chili taste without the use of meat. The following recipe has an excellent blend of vegetables and spices to yield a delicious chili that, for vegetarians, packs a wallop.

2–3 cups pinto beans, soaked overnight in water
2–3 teaspoons salt
2 tablespoons olive oil
2 onions, chopped
4 garlic cloves, minced
3 celery stalks, chopped
3 carrots, chopped
4 tomatoes, peeled and chopped
6 tablespoons chili powder
1 teaspoon cumin
½ teaspoon oregano
1 teaspoon basil
½–1 teaspoon ground black pepper
1–2 green bell peppers, chopped
1 cup tomato juice
1 cup cracked wheat

Drain pinto beans, transfer to a cooking pot, cover with fresh water, add 1 teaspoon salt, and bring to a boil for 1 minute. Lower heat to simmer, and cook beans until tender, approximately 2 hours. Heat olive oil in a large pot, add onions and garlic, and sauté. When onions are translucent, add celery, carrots, tomatoes, the remaining salt, and the other spices. Cover and cook over medium heat for 15 minutes or until vegetables are tender. Add bell peppers and cook another 10 minutes. In a separate saucepan, bring tomato juice to a boil. Remove from heat, add cracked wheat, stir, and let sit for 5 minutes. Add pinto beans (with water) and cracked wheat to pot, stir well, and simmer for 30 minutes. Add water if needed, and adjust seasonings for taste.

# POOR MAN'S VEGETARIAN CHILI

Lorenzo Borrego, who provided this recipe, is a seventy-five-year-old vegetarian who lives on a tight budget. Following years of trial and error, he arrived at this recipe, which is inexpensive, nutritious, and easy to prepare.

4–5 8-ounce cans tomato sauce
1 6-ounce can tomato paste
1 cup mushrooms, chopped
1 red bell pepper, chopped
2–3 jalapeno peppers, stemmed and diced
1 onion, chopped
Salt to taste
Crushed red pepper to taste
6 tablespoons chili powder
1 tablespoon cumin
2 garlic cloves, minced
1 teaspoon oregano
½ teaspoon allspice
1 cup textured soy protein

In a large cooking pot, combine tomato sauce, tomato paste, mushrooms, bell pepper, jalapenos, onion, salt, red pepper, chili powder, cumin, garlic, oregano, and allspice. Stir, add soy, and bring to a boil. Boil for 1 minute, lower heat, and simmer for 1½–2 hours. Serve with sourdough bread and iced tea.

# SALT-FREE CHILI

For those who must remain cautious about their salt intake, the following recipe deserves a try.

1 tablespoon olive oil
3 medium onions, chopped
1 green bell pepper, chopped
1–1½ pounds lean beef, cubed
2 garlic cloves, minced
2 tablespoons ground red chile, hot
1 tablespoon ground red chile, mild
1 teaspoon cumin
1 teaspoon oregano
½ teaspoon pepper
4 cups salt-free canned tomatoes
1 tablespoon red wine vinegar

Heat oil in a cast-iron skillet, add onions and bell peppers, and sauté. When onions are translucent, add beef, garlic, chiles, cumin, and oregano, stirring well. When meat is browned, add pepper, tomatoes, and vinegar. Simmer for at least 1 hour, stirring occasionally. Add seasonings for taste.

# SCALLOP CHILI

Scallops are a tiny yet tasty marine bivalve, and they provide the essential flavor and texture for this exotic dish.

4 tablespoons unsalted butter
3 tablespoons olive oil
1 shallot, chopped
2 garlic cloves, minced
4 fresh Anaheim chiles, stemmed, seeded, peeled, and chopped
2 red or green bell peppers, chopped
2 pounds scallops
1 fresh lime
Salt and pepper to taste

In a large cast-iron skillet, heat butter and oil. Sauté shallot, garlic, chile peppers, and bell peppers. Add scallops and cook over medium heat for another 5 minutes. Squeeze juice from lime into skillet, and salt and pepper to taste. Serve with steamed rice.

# SHITAKE AND WHITE MUSHROOM CHILI

The blend of shitake and white mushrooms offers a flavor quite different from most of the recipes in this section.

2 tablespoons olive oil
1 large onion, chopped
2 garlic cloves, minced
3 tablespoons chili powder
1 teaspoon cumin
½ pound fresh shitake mushrooms, chopped
1½ pounds fresh white mushrooms, chopped
1 14½-ounce can stewed tomatoes
1 19-ounce can white beans, drained
½ cup water

In a large cooking pot, heat olive oil, add onion and garlic, and sauté. Add chili powder and cumin and cook for an additional 2 minutes, stirring frequently. Add mushrooms and cook for another 6–7 minutes. Add tomatoes, beans, and water. Stir and simmer for 10 minutes. Serve topped with fresh chopped parsley or cilantro.

# SHRIMP CHILI

Unlike chili made from beef and other meats, shrimp chili doesn't need much simmering time and can be ready to eat only minutes after beginning preparation.

4 tablespoons cooking oil
2 medium onions, chopped
4 garlic cloves, minced
4 Anaheim chiles, stemmed, seeded, and diced
1 pound fresh shrimp, peeled
¼ cup fresh cilantro, chopped
¼ cup fresh parsley, chopped
Salt and white pepper to taste

In a large cast-iron skillet, heat oil. Sauté onions, garlic, and chiles. Add shrimp, stir, and cook for another 2–3 minutes. Add cilantro, parsley, salt, and pepper and cook for an additional 2 minutes. Delicious served over rice.

# SKINNY MINNIE CHILI

Minnie Mendoza claims she lost eight pounds eating nothing but one serving of this chili per day over a three-month period.

2 tablespoons olive oil
1 large onion, chopped
½ celery stalk, chopped
1 green bell pepper, chopped
½ cup mushrooms, sliced
2 pounds boneless chicken breasts, cubed
3 tablespoons chili powder
½ teaspoon oregano
1 teaspoon cumin
3 garlic cloves, minced
Salt to taste
1 16-ounce can tomatoes
1 6-ounce can tomato paste
1 4-ounce can green chiles

Heat oil in a cooking pot and sauté onion, celery, and bell pepper. Add mushrooms and cook for another 5 minutes. Add chicken, chili powder, oregano, cumin, and garlic. Stir well, and cook until meat is browned. Add remaining ingredients, bring to a boil, reduce heat, and simmer for 1–1½ hours, stirring occasionally.

# SLIM'S DIET CHILI

Slim Whittaker was a West Texas cowhand who professed to love chili more than life itself. After Slim's weight ballooned to over 250 pounds on his 5'7" frame, he started cutting down on portions of chili and experimented with leaner ingredients. The result follows, with a total calorie count of less than 250 per bowl.

1 tablespoon olive oil
2 onions, chopped
1 garlic clove, minced
1½–2 pounds very lean beef, coarsely ground
3 tablespoons chili powder
1 teaspoon Mexican oregano
1–2 teaspoons cumin
Salt to taste
4–5 fresh tomatoes, peeled and chopped
3–4 4-ounce cans chopped green chiles

Heat oil in a large cast-iron skillet, add onions and garlic, and sauté. Add meat, chili powder, oregano, cumin, and salt. Stir well, and cook until meat is browned. Add tomatoes and green chiles and a bit of water. Bring to a boil, lower heat, and simmer for at least 1 hour, stirring occasionally and adding water if necessary. Let sit overnight in the refrigerator. When ready to serve, skim any congealed grease off top, heat, and ladle into bowls.

# SOYBEAN CHILI #1

Soybeans are making serious inroads into all kinds of recipes. They inevitably found their way into the chili pot.

1 tablespoon olive oil
2 medium onions, chopped
5–6 garlic cloves, minced
1 14½-ounce can chopped tomatoes
1 tablespoon oregano
1 tablespoon cumin
1 tablespoon chili powder
2 cups cooked soybeans

Heat olive oil in a skillet and sauté onions and garlic for about 5 minutes. Lower heat slightly, add tomatoes, and cook for an additional 5 minutes. Add oregano, cumin, and chili powder. Stir well and cook for another 3 minutes. Add soybeans, bring to a boil, reduce heat, and simmer for 45 minutes.

# SOYBEAN CHILI #2

This recipe is the result of a couple of years of tinkering with ingredients and testing it on friends.

2 tablespoons olive oil
2 teaspoons cumin
2 medium onions, chopped
6–8 ounces tempeh (soybean product found in health food stores)
1 tablespoon minced garlic
1 green bell pepper, diced
1 red bell pepper, diced
2 tablespoons chili powder
2 teaspoons oregano
3 ancho chiles, stemmed, seeded, and diced
Salt to taste
1 bottle dark Mexican beer
2 cans tomatoes, chopped
2 cups cooked soybeans
3–4 tablespoons fresh cilantro, chopped

Heat oil in a skillet, add cumin, and sauté for a few seconds. Add onions and tempeh, and sauté until onions are translucent. Add garlic, bell peppers, chili powder, oregano, chile peppers, and salt to taste. Sauté for another 1–2 minutes, stirring constantly. Add beer, tomatoes, and soybeans. Bring to a boil, cover, reduce heat, and simmer for 30 minutes. Before serving, add cilantro and stir well.

# TEXAS PENICILLIN

This recipe is called Texas Penicillin because, according to the creator, it is a sure cure for everything that ails you, including broken hearts.

2 pounds boneless chicken breasts, cubed
2 cans low-salt chicken stock
1 14-ounce can Italian-style diced tomatoes
3 garlic cloves, minced
1 medium zucchini, sliced thinly
1 medium carrot, sliced thinly
1 large red pepper, chopped
1 14-ounce can sweet corn
1 15-ounce can Ranch Style beans
2–3 tablespoons chili powder
1½–2 tablespoons cumin
4 green onions, chopped
½ cup fresh cilantro, chopped

Place chicken in a large pot with chicken stock, tomatoes, and garlic. Bring to a boil, reduce heat, and simmer for 20 minutes. Add the fresh vegetables and simmer for an additional 10 minutes. Add canned vegetables and remaining spices, and simmer another 10 minutes. Remove from heat, add green onions and cilantro, and serve with crusty bread and a mixed green salad with honey-mustard dressing.

# VEGETARIAN CHILI #1

The following is one of the simplest and quickest recipes in this entire book.

3 cups water
1 15½-ounce can Ranch Style beans
1 14½-ounce can diced tomatoes
1 11½-ounce can Snap-E-Tom tomato juice
1 medium onion, chopped
1 4½-ounce can chopped green chiles
½ cup uncooked long grain rice
2 teaspoons cumin

In a large cooking pot, combine all ingredients, bring to a boil, reduce heat, cover, and allow to simmer for 20 minutes or until rice is done.

# VEGETARIAN CHILI #2

1–2 tablespoons cooking oil
2 garlic cloves, minced
2 tablespoons chili powder
1 teaspoon cumin
1 teaspoon oregano
½ teaspoon pepper
2 cups green beans
2–3 carrots, finely chopped
4–5 celery stalks, chopped
1 15-ounce can tomatoes
1 cup water
1 onion, chopped
2 green or red bell peppers, chopped
2 New Mexico green chiles, peeled and chopped
1 can pinto beans
Salt to taste

In a large cooking pot, heat oil. Add garlic, chili powder, cumin, oregano, and pepper, and cook for 2 minutes. Add green beans, carrots, celery, tomatoes, and water. Bring to a boil, reduce heat, and simmer for 15 minutes. Add onion, bell peppers, green chiles, pinto beans, and salt to taste; cook an additional 10–15 minutes. Adjust seasonings to taste.

# VEGETARIAN CHILI WITH CHICKEN

1 tablespoon olive oil

1 pound chicken, skinned, boned, and cubed

1 onion, chopped

1 green bell pepper, chopped

2–3 jalapeno peppers, chopped

2–3 garlic cloves, minced

¼ cup sun-dried tomatoes

2 tablespoons chili powder

1 tablespoon cumin

2 teaspoons oregano

Salt and pepper to taste

2 cups water

1 cup dried pinto beans, soaked overnight in salt water and drained

1 cup fresh tomato, chopped

1 cup fresh corn

In a skillet, heat oil and brown chicken. Add onion, bell pepper, jalapenos, and garlic, and sauté. Add tomatoes, chili powder, cumin, oregano, salt, and pepper. Stir well and cook for 1 minute. Add water and beans, stir again, bring to a boil, reduce heat, and simmer for 1½ hours. Add fresh tomato and corn and continue simmering another 30 minutes or until pinto beans are tender.

# VEGETARIAN CHILI WITH A ZING

The addition of lots of jalapeno peppers along with spicy Bloody Mary mix gives this version of chili an extra zing.

1 cup cracked wheat
1 cup spicy Bloody Mary mix
2 tablespoons olive oil
2 medium onions, chopped
2 garlic cloves, minced
2 celery stalks, chopped
4–6 tablespoons chili powder
1 teaspoon oregano
1 28-ounce can tomatoes
2 cups water
2 green or red bell peppers, chopped
4–5 jalapeno peppers, chopped
2 packages frozen green beans
2 cans pinto beans, drained
2 cans garbanzo beans, drained
1 can corn, drained
Salt, pepper, and cayenne pepper to taste

Allow cracked wheat to soak in Bloody Mary mix for 1 hour. Heat oil in a large cooking pot. Sauté onions, garlic, and celery. Add chili powder, oregano, tomatoes, and water. Stir, bring to a boil, reduce heat, and simmer for 30 minutes. Add bell peppers and jalapenos, and cook for another 15–20 minutes. Add green beans and cracked wheat, stir, and cook an additional 20 minutes, stirring frequently. Add pinto beans, garbanzos, and corn, and cook another 15 minutes. Add salt, pepper, and cayenne to taste, and serve.

# WHEAT CHILI

"Wheat, not meat!" claims a chili-loving friend who came up with the following recipe in response to a doctor's order to lose fifty pounds. In spite of the title, this recipe contains a pound of lean beef. Aside from the addition of whole wheat kernels, this recipe contains, for the most part, many of the traditional ingredients expected in a great bowl of chili.

1 cup whole wheat kernels
2 tablespoons olive oil
2 onions, chopped
1 pound very lean beef, cubed
3–4 tablespoons chili powder
3 garlic cloves, minced
½ teaspoon oregano
2 teaspoons cumin
Salt to taste
½ teaspoon crushed red pepper
1 8-ounce can green chiles
1 8-ounce can tomato paste
1 32-ounce can tomato juice

Soak wheat kernels overnight in water. The next day, place the wheat, along with the water in which it was soaked, in a saucepan and bring to a boil. Heat oil in a large skillet, add onions, and sauté. In a separate bowl, combine beef, chili powder, garlic, oregano, cumin, and salt. Mix well, add to skillet, stir, and cook until meat is browned. Add red pepper, green chiles, tomato paste, and tomato juice. Drain wheat and save liquid. Add wheat to skillet and stir, bring to a boil, reduce heat, and simmer for 1 hour. Add more of the liquid when necessary. Serve with a tossed green salad.

# about the author

**W. C. Jameson** is the award-winning author of 45 books and over 1500 articles and essays. When he is not working on a book, he travels the country speaking at writers' conferences and conducting seminars in writing and poetry.

In addition to having earned his living as a ranch hand, disc jockey, dock worker, lifeguard, boxer, musician, college professor, and writer, Jameson is a songwriter who performs regularly at folk festivals, colleges and universities, roadhouses, and concert halls, playing the music from his four successful CDs.

When he is not on the road, Jameson relaxes at his Woodland Park, Colorado, home cooking and preparing new recipes.